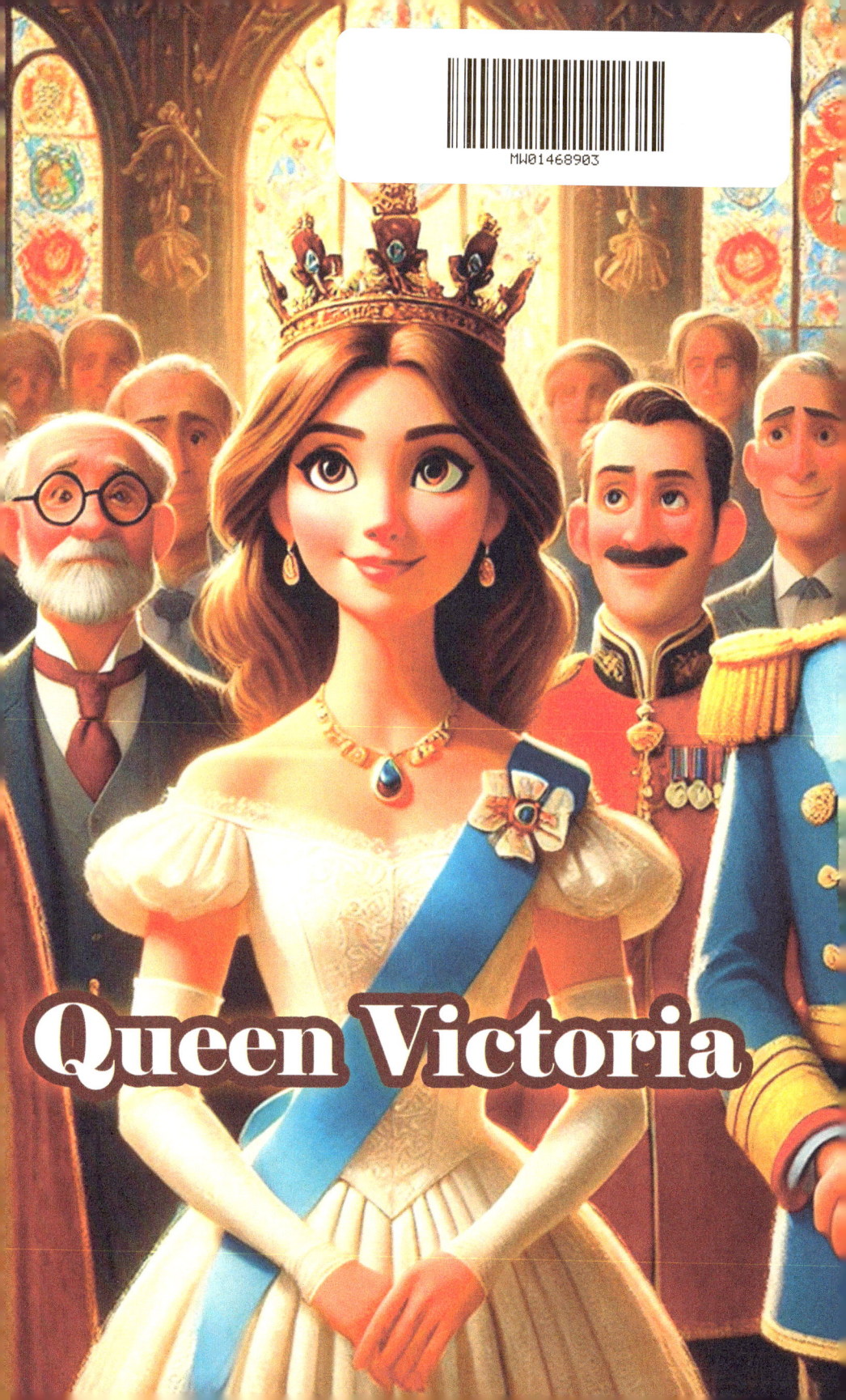

Queen Victoria

Contents

The Life of Queen Victoria —————————————— 3

Chapter 1: The Little Princess —————————————— 6

Chapter 2: A Surprise for Victoria —————————————— 20

Chapter 3: The Day She Became Queen —————————————— 32

Chapter 4: A Young Queen's First Decisions —————————————— 44

Chapter 5: A Love Story - Victoria and Albert —————————————— 57

Chapter 6: The Great Exhibition —————————————— 70

Chapter 7: A Time of Sadness —————————————— 84

Chapter 8: The Widow of Windsor —————————————— 95

Chapter 9: Empress of India —————————————— 105

Chapter 10: The Golden Jubilee —————————————— 118

Chapter 11: The Final Years and Legacy —————————————— 129

Timelines —————————————— 140

The Life of Queen Victoria

"Great events make me quiet and calm; it is only trifles that irritate my nerves."
Queen Victoria

Hello, young readers! Are you ready to learn about a queen who ruled over a vast empire and became one of the most famous queens in history? Let me introduce you to Queen Victoria who ruled the United Kingdom for over 60 years!

Queen Victoria was born in 1819 in London, England. When she was a little girl, no one expected her to become queen so young. But when she was just 18 years old, she was crowned Queen of the United Kingdom. Even though she was young, she took her role very seriously and worked hard to be a good leader.

Victoria's reign, known as the Victorian Era, was a time of great change and progress. It was a period when new inventions, such as the steam engine and the telephone, transformed the way people lived. Britain became the most powerful country in the world, and its empire spread across many continents.

Queen Victoria was not just a powerful ruler; she was also a loving wife and mother. She married Prince Albert, and together they had nine children. They were very close, and their family life was important to Victoria.

However, Victoria's life was not always easy. She faced many challenges and losses, but she remained strong and dedicated to her people. She became known as the "Grandmother of Europe" because many of her children married into other royal families across Europe.

In this book, you'll journey through the fascinating life of Queen Victoria, from her early days as a young queen to her time as the beloved matriarch of a vast empire. You'll discover how she helped shape a new era and why she is remembered as one of the greatest queens in history.

So, let's step back in time and explore the incredible life of Queen Victoria, the queen who ruled an empire and left a lasting legacy!

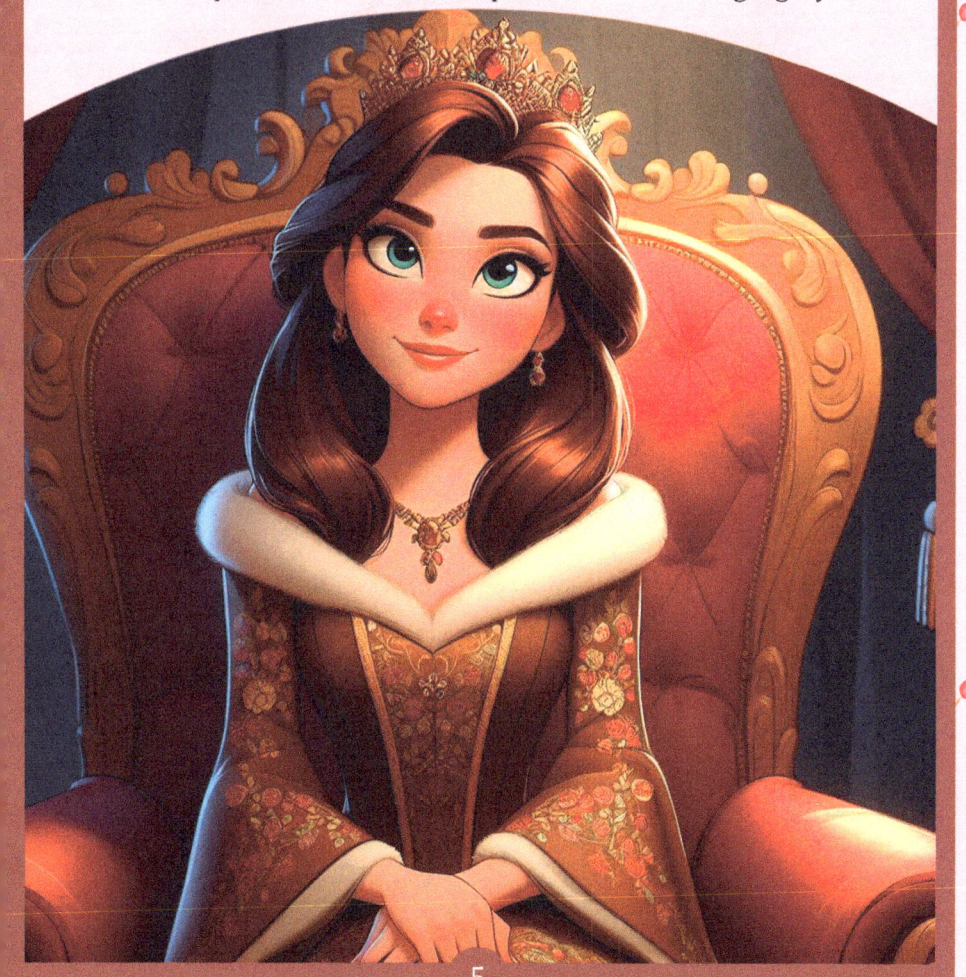

The Little Princess

"The important thing is not what they think of me, but what I think of them."
Queen Victoria

Once upon a time, in a grand palace in London called Kensington Palace, a little princess was born. Her name was Victoria, and she came into the world on May 24, 1819. The palace was a big, beautiful place with tall towers, grand staircases, and lovely gardens full of flowers. Inside the palace, everyone was excited to welcome the new baby princess.

Princess Victoria was the daughter of Prince Edward, who was a tall, kind man with a warm smile. Her mother was Princess Victoria of Saxe-Coburg-Saalfeld, a gentle lady who always took care of her little girl. The young princess was the joy of her parents' lives, and they loved her very much.

As Victoria grew older, she loved to play with her dolls. She had many dolls, each with its own special dress and tiny shoes. She would line them up and pretend they were her royal court, giving them names and stories of their own. The dolls were her closest friends, and she spent hours playing with them in her nursery.

But Victoria's life wasn't just about playing. From a young age, she had to learn many important things. Every day, a kind lady called a governess would come to teach her. This governess, named Baroness Lehzen, was very wise and taught Victoria how to read, write, and do sums. They would sit by the window, where sunlight streamed in, and Victoria would carefully trace letters on her slate or read stories from her favorite books. Victoria loved learning, especially when the lessons were about faraway lands or brave knights and princesses. She would listen with wide eyes, imagining herself in those magical places. But there were also times when the lessons were hard, and Victoria had to concentrate very hard to understand. Even when things were difficult, she always tried her best because she knew how important it was to learn. Even though she was a princess, Victoria's life was not as grand as one might think. She wasn't expected to become a queen. You see, Victoria had many uncles, and they were all older than her, so everyone thought one of their children would be the next king or queen. This meant that Victoria could enjoy being a little girl, without the heavy responsibilities of ruling a kingdom.

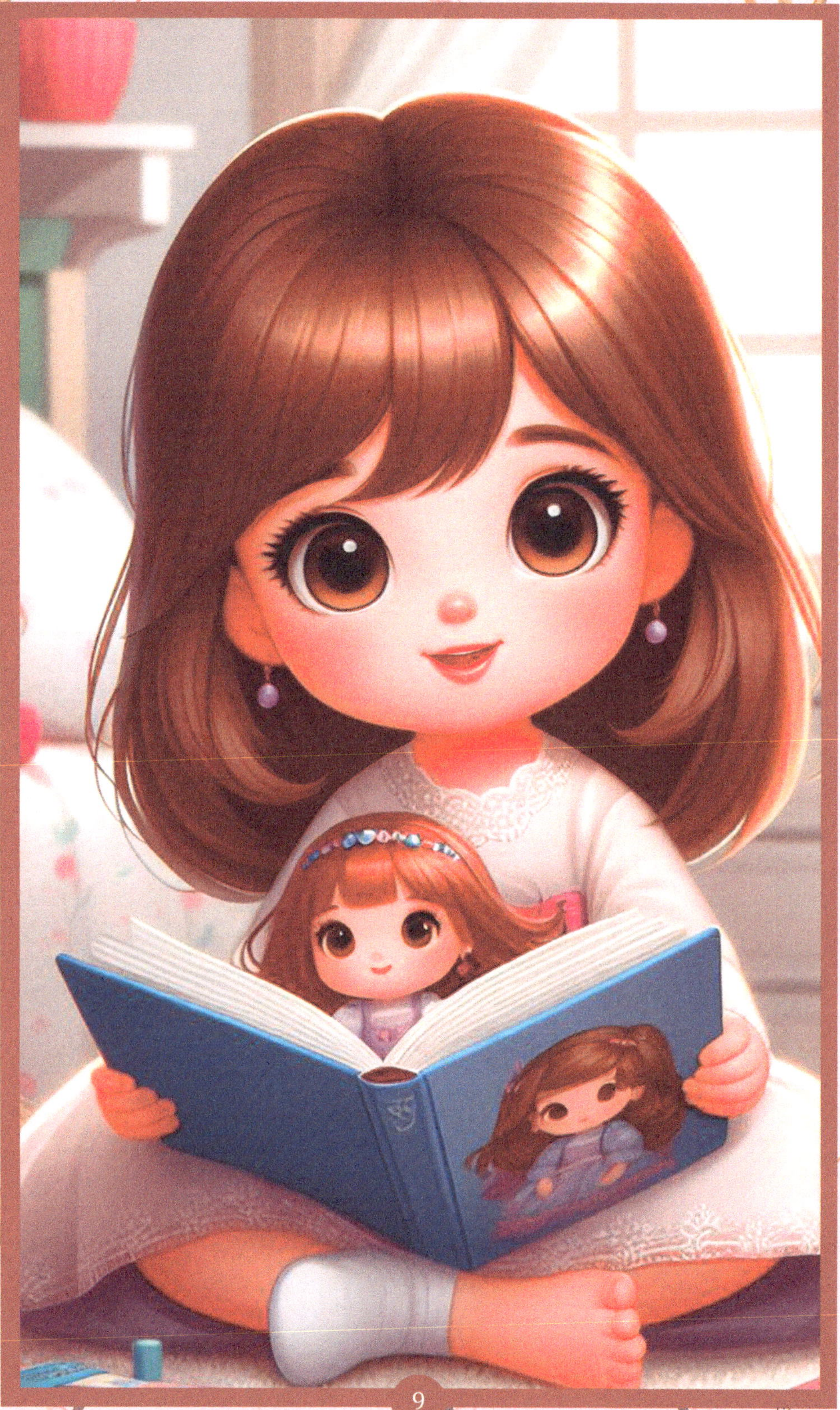

But Victoria was special, even if she didn't know it yet. She was smart, curious, and full of energy. Every morning, she would wake up early, eager to explore the palace gardens. She loved to pick flowers, chase butterflies, and listen to the birds singing in the trees. The palace staff would often see her running around, her cheeks rosy with excitement, and her laughter echoing through the halls.

Victoria's life at Kensington Palace was happy and peaceful. She didn't know what the future held for her, and she didn't worry about it. For now, she was just a little princess with a big imagination, living in a world of her own, surrounded by people who loved her.

And so, the little princess played, learned, and dreamed, not knowing that one day, her life would change in a way she could never have imagined. But for now, Victoria was simply a little girl, with her dolls, her books, and her endless curiosity about the world around her.

Fascinating Facts about Young Victoria:

Victoria's Name - When Victoria was born, her parents gave her a long name: Alexandrina Victoria. This was a very special name because it combined names from different parts of her family. But because "Alexandrina Victoria" is quite a long name, her family gave her a shorter, sweeter nickname to use every day. They called her "Drina," which was easier to say and sounded cute for a little girl.

As a baby and a little girl, Drina lived in Kensington Palace with her mother, the Duchess of Kent, and other people who helped take care of her. She didn't know it yet, but one day, she would grow up to become the queen of a very large country! But for now, she was just a little girl with a special nickname, living in a big palace.

Strict Upbringing - When Victoria was a little girl, her life was very strict and carefully planned out by her mother, the Duchess of Kent, and a man named Sir John Conroy, who worked closely with her mother. They created a special set of rules called the "Kensington System" to raise Victoria in a very specific way.

The Kensington System was like a strict schedule that Victoria had to follow every day. She wasn't allowed to do many of the things that other children could do. For example, she couldn't play with other kids her age or even go out and explore on her own. Instead, she had to stay inside the palace most of the time, and she was always watched very closely.

The idea behind the Kensington System was to keep Victoria isolated, which means she was kept away from other people and children. Her mother and Sir John Conroy wanted to make sure she only listened to them and did what they wanted. They thought that by controlling everything in her life, they could make sure she would grow up to be a queen who would do what they told her to do.

Because of this system, Victoria had a very lonely childhood. She didn't have many friends, and she was always under the watchful eyes of her mother and Conroy. But even though her life was strict and controlled, Victoria grew up to be strong and independent, ready to take on her role as queen one day.

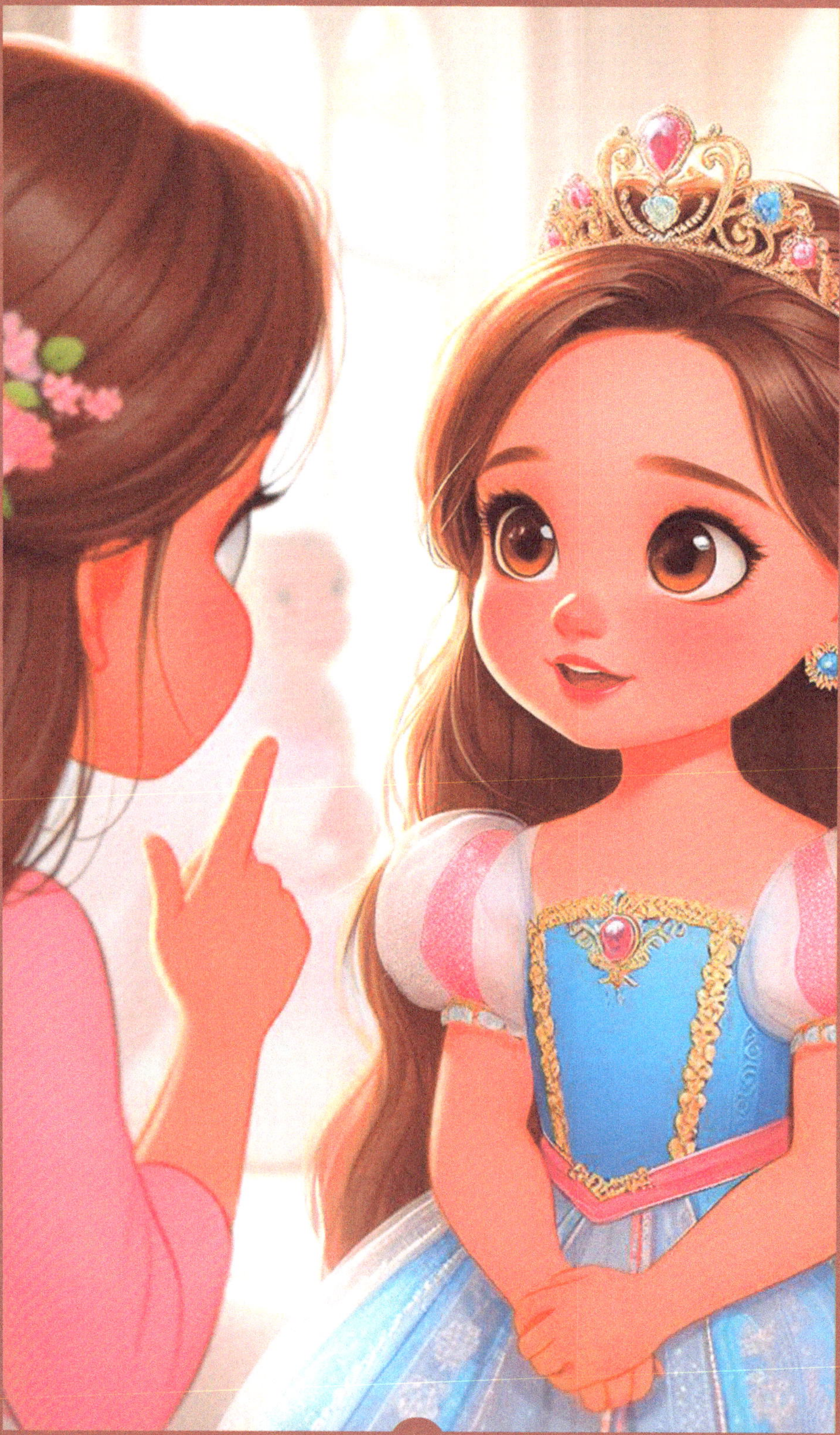

Close Relationship with Her Governess - Queen Victoria had a very special person in her life when she was a young girl, and that person was her governess, Baroness Louise Lehzen. A governess is like a teacher who lives with you and helps you learn about many different things. Baroness Lehzen was a noblewoman from Germany, which means she came from a family that was important and respected.

Lehzen wasn't just a teacher to Victoria; she was like a second mother and a close friend. Because Victoria's life was so strict and controlled by her mother and Sir John Conroy, she didn't have many people she could talk to or share her feelings with. But with Lehzen, Victoria felt safe and understood. Lehzen listened to her, comforted her when she was sad, and helped her with her lessons.

Lehzen taught Victoria about many subjects, like history, languages, and how to behave properly as a princess. But she also taught Victoria about important values, like the importance of being responsible, doing the right thing, and caring for others. Lehzen believed that Victoria should be strong and independent, and she encouraged her to think for herself.

Because of Lehzen's influence, Victoria grew up with a strong sense of duty, meaning she understood that she had important responsibilities as a future queen. Lehzen's support helped Victoria become confident and prepared for the big role she would one day take on as the Queen of England.

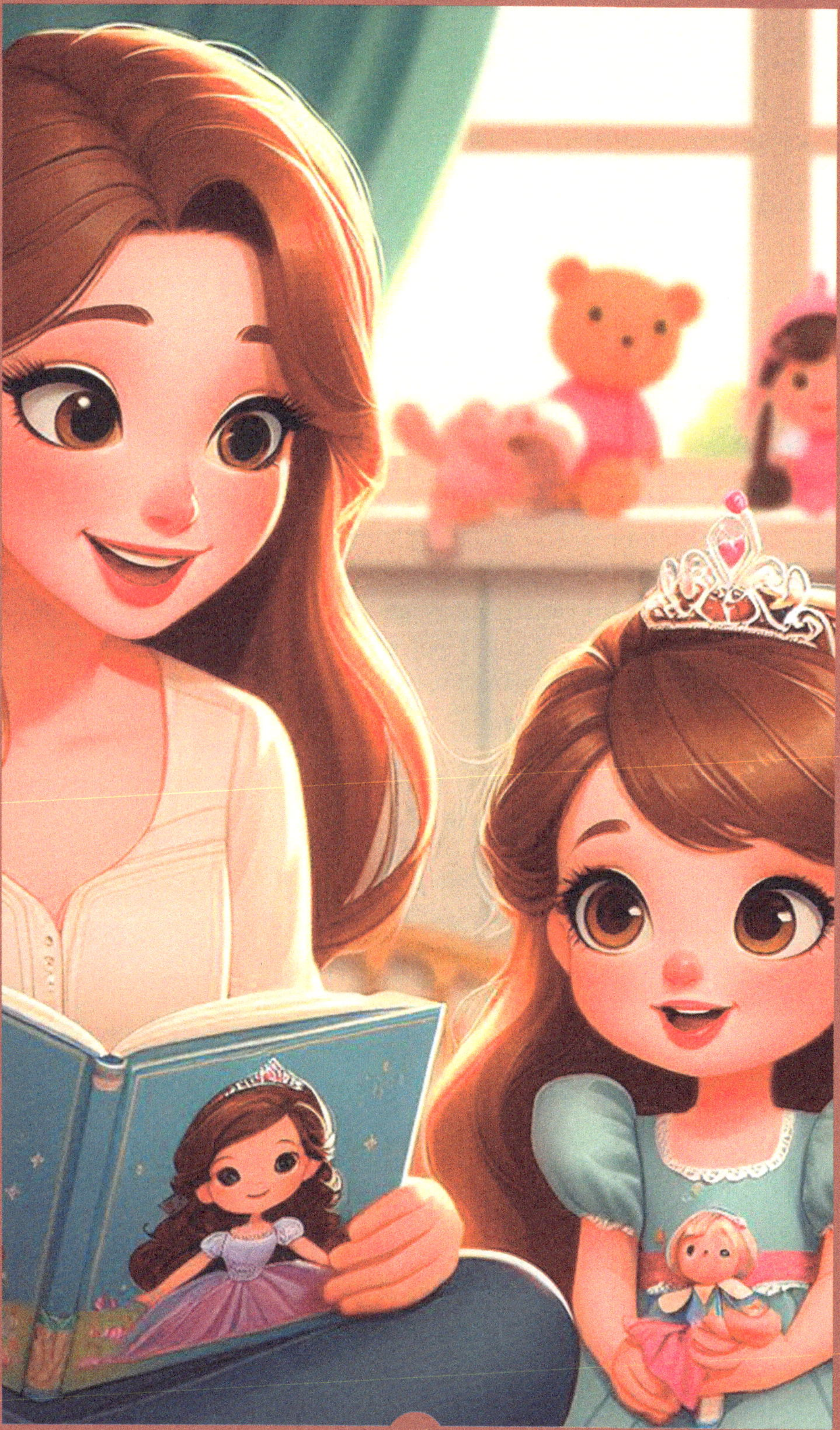

A Resilient Spirit - Even though Queen Victoria's childhood was very strict and controlled by her mother and Sir John Conroy, she showed a lot of strength and determination. The rules and schedules of her upbringing were meant to make her follow exactly what her mother and Conroy wanted, but Victoria had a strong will of her own.

From a young age, Victoria was known for being very independent and determined. Even though she was often kept away from other children and had to follow many rules, she didn't always agree with the way things were done. For example, she sometimes resisted the control of her mother and Conroy, showing that she had her own ideas about how things should be.

This spirit of standing up for herself and wanting to make her own choices was a big part of who Victoria was. As she grew older, these traits became even more important. When she eventually became queen, she used her strong will and independence to make decisions and lead her country in her own way.

Victoria's ability to resist control and her clear sense of what she wanted helped her become a powerful and respected queen. Her resilient spirit, which started to show in her childhood, defined her entire reign and made her one of the most famous and influential monarchs in history.

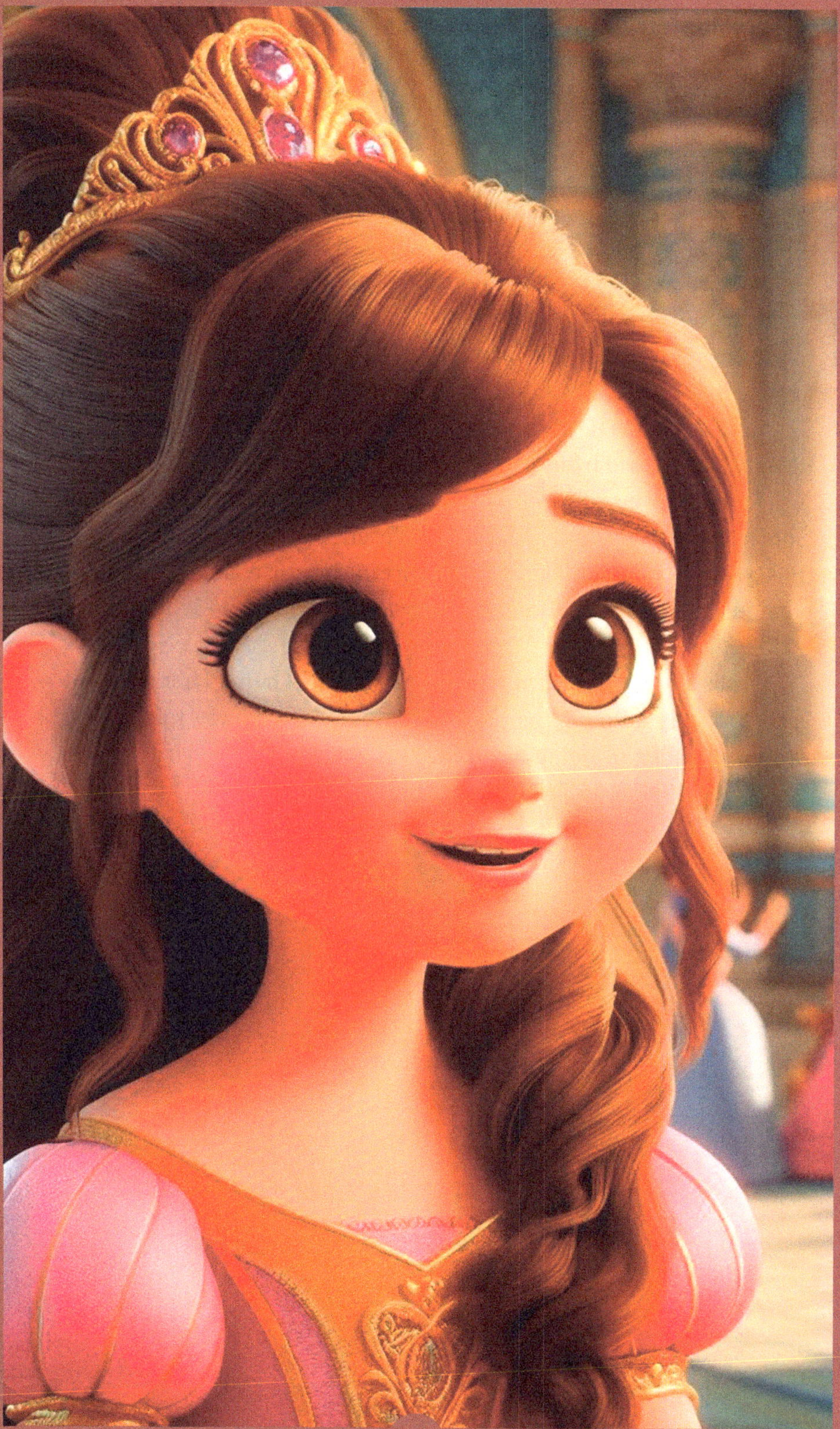

Early Education - Queen Victoria had a very thorough and serious education when she was a young girl. This means she learned a lot of different subjects and had to study hard every day. Her education was designed to prepare her for her important future as the Queen of England.

Victoria's lessons included many subjects. She learned about languages, which are the different ways people speak in other countries. She became very good at speaking both English and German because her family was from both England and Germany. But she didn't stop there—she also studied French, Italian, and Latin, which is an old language that was spoken by the Romans.

Victoria also learned about history, where she studied important events and people from the past. This helped her understand how the world had changed over time. Geography was another important subject, where she learned about different countries, places, and how the world is shaped. This was important because, as a future queen, she needed to know about the lands and people she would one day rule.

Victoria's education was very demanding, but it helped her grow into a smart, well-rounded person who was ready to take on the responsibilities of being a queen. And despite all the hard work, she always made time for the things she loved, like art.

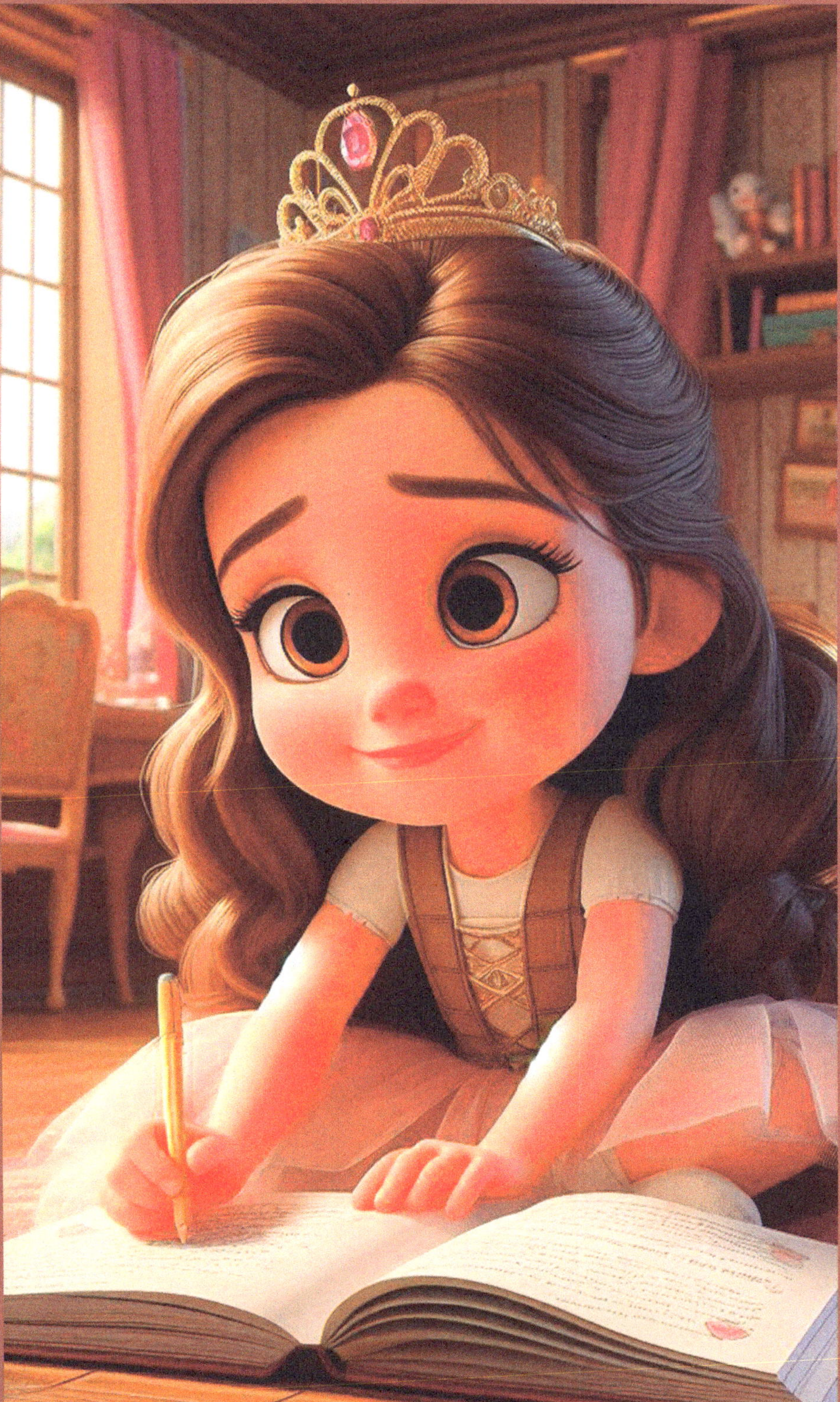

A Surprise for Victoria

"I think it is very good for children to learn to be strong and to endure."
Queen Victoria

Victoria was a happy little girl who loved playing in the gardens and learning new things. She lived in a grand palace, surrounded by people who cared for her. But there was something Victoria didn't know—something very important about her future.

When Victoria was just a baby, her father, Prince Edward, passed away. It was a sad time for her family, but Victoria was too young to understand what had happened. Her mother, Princess Victoria, took care of her with all the love she could give. As Victoria grew older, she spent her days playing with her dolls, reading books, and learning from her kind governess, Baroness Lehzen.

Victoria knew that she was a princess, but she didn't know what that really meant. She didn't know that her uncles, who were all kings and princes, didn't have any children who could become the next king or queen. As the years passed, something incredible happened—Victoria became the next in line to the throne! But nobody told her yet. They wanted to wait until she was a little older.

One sunny morning, when Victoria was just 11 years old, something very special happened. Her mother called her into a big room where important people were waiting. Victoria felt a little nervous, but she was also curious. What could this be about?

As she entered the room, everyone smiled at her. Her mother gently took her hand and said, "Victoria, my dear, there is something very important we need to tell you."

Victoria looked up at her mother with wide eyes. "What is it, Mama?" she asked.

Her mother knelt down to be at eye level with Victoria. "One day, you are going to be Queen," she said softly.

Victoria blinked in surprise. "Queen? Me?"

"Yes, my darling," her mother replied. "Because your uncles don't have any children, you are next in line to be the ruler of our country. One day, you will be Queen Victoria."

For a moment, Victoria didn't know what to say. She felt a mix of emotions—surprise, excitement, and even a little bit of fear. She had always loved stories about queens and princesses, but she never imagined that she would be one herself!

"But, Mama," Victoria said quietly, "being a queen sounds very important. What if I'm not ready?"

Her mother smiled warmly. "That's why we will help you prepare, my dear. You have always worked hard in your lessons, and now you will have even more to learn. But don't worry—you will have time, and we

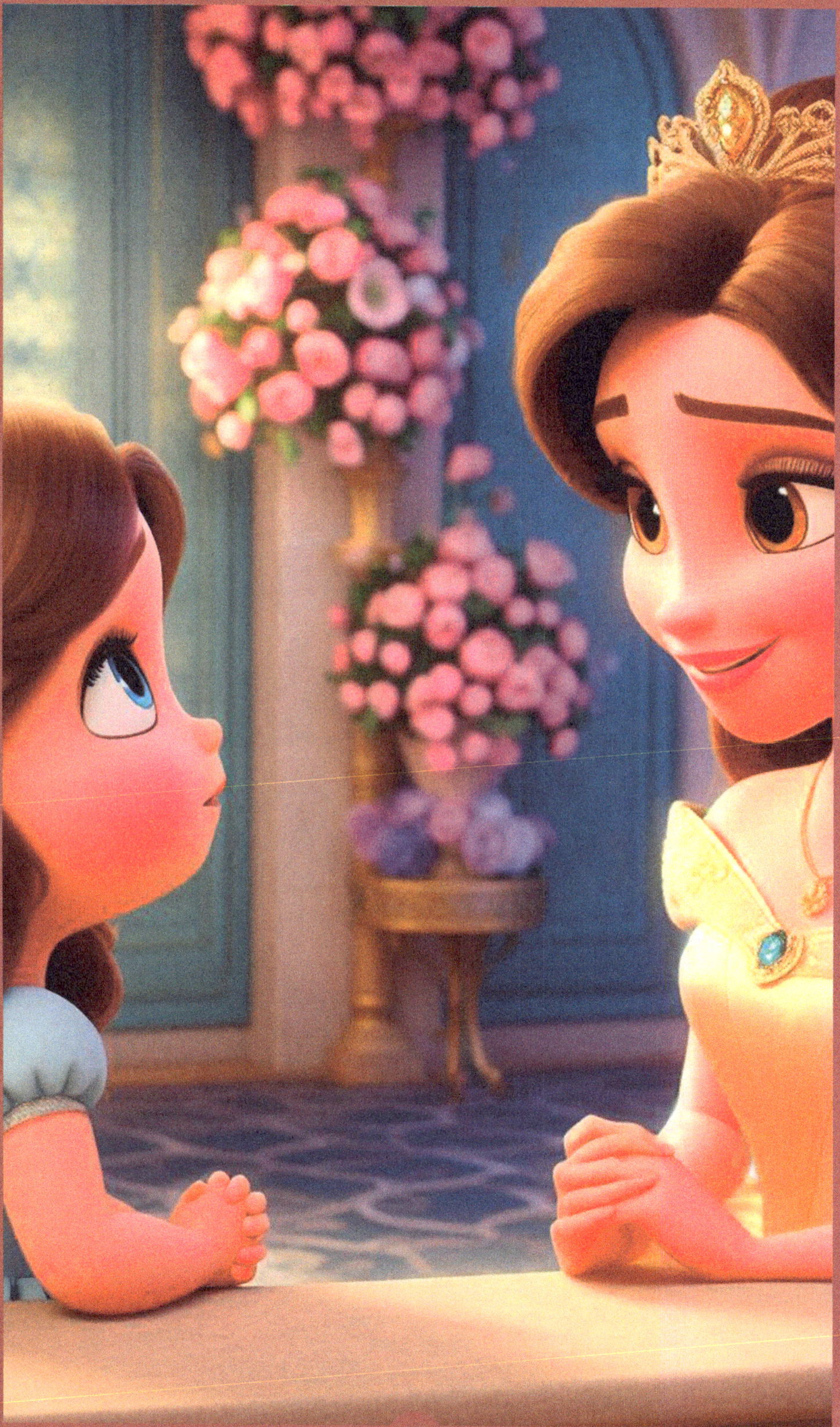

From that day on, Victoria took her lessons even more seriously. She studied history, learned about the people she would one day lead, and practiced speaking with confidence. She knew that being a queen was a big responsibility, but she was determined to do her best.

Even though the idea of becoming queen was a little scary, Victoria felt proud too. She knew she would have the chance to help people and make her country a better place. And deep down, she knew she could do it, as long as she kept learning and working hard.

Victoria was still a young girl with a big heart and a lot to learn. But now, she knew that one day, she would wear a crown and be called Queen Victoria. And while that day was still far away, she was ready to begin her journey toward becoming a great queen.

Fascinating Facts about Young Victoria:

Her Father's Early Death - When Queen Victoria was just a tiny baby, only eight months old, something very sad happened—her father, the Duke of Kent, passed away. This meant that Victoria never really got to know her father because she was so young when he died.

After her father's death, Victoria's life changed a lot. Her mother, the Duchess of Kent, had to take care of Victoria all by herself. Because they didn't have the Duke anymore, Victoria and her mother were not included as much in the royal family's activities and events. This means they were left out of many important gatherings at the royal court, where the king and other important people would meet.

Feeling left out and worried about Victoria's future, her mother became very protective. She wanted to make sure that Victoria would grow up to be a strong and capable queen, but she also wanted to have control over everything Victoria did. This is why her mother, with the help of Sir John Conroy, created the strict "Kensington System" to control how Victoria was raised.

Because her father wasn't there to protect her and guide her, Victoria's mother took charge of her upbringing, making sure that Victoria followed all the rules and stayed close to her. This made Victoria's childhood very different from that of other children, as she had to live a very controlled and isolated life.

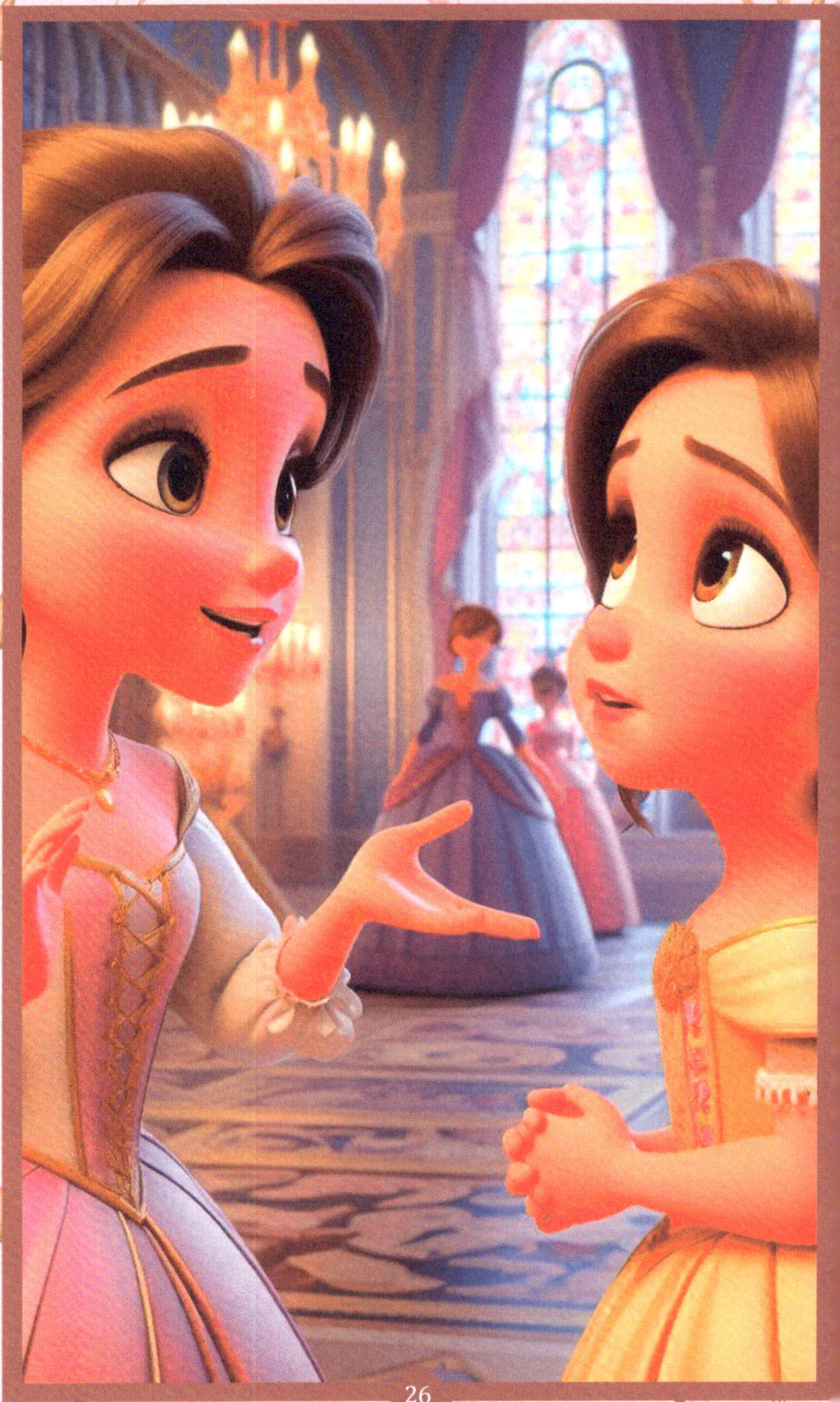

Sense of Destiny - When Queen Victoria was a young girl, she didn't know right away that she would one day become the queen. But as she got older, she started to learn about her special place in the royal family and what that meant for her future.

One day, when Victoria was about 13 years old, something very important happened. Her governess, Baroness Lehzen, showed her a special chart called a genealogical chart. This chart was like a big family tree that showed all the people in Victoria's family and how they were related to each other. As Victoria looked at the chart, she suddenly realized something very big: she was next in line to become the queen!

This was a huge moment for Victoria. She understood that one day, she would have the enormous responsibility of leading the whole country. Even though she was still just a young girl, she knew that being a queen was a very important job.

According to a famous story, when Victoria realized that she would be queen, she didn't panic or get scared. Instead, she calmly said, "I will be good." This simple sentence showed that Victoria already had a strong sense of duty and responsibility. She knew that being a queen would mean making good decisions and doing her best for her people.

This moment marked the beginning of Victoria understanding her destiny—the special future that was waiting for her. Even though she was still young, she was determined to be a good queen, and she carried this promise with her throughout her life.

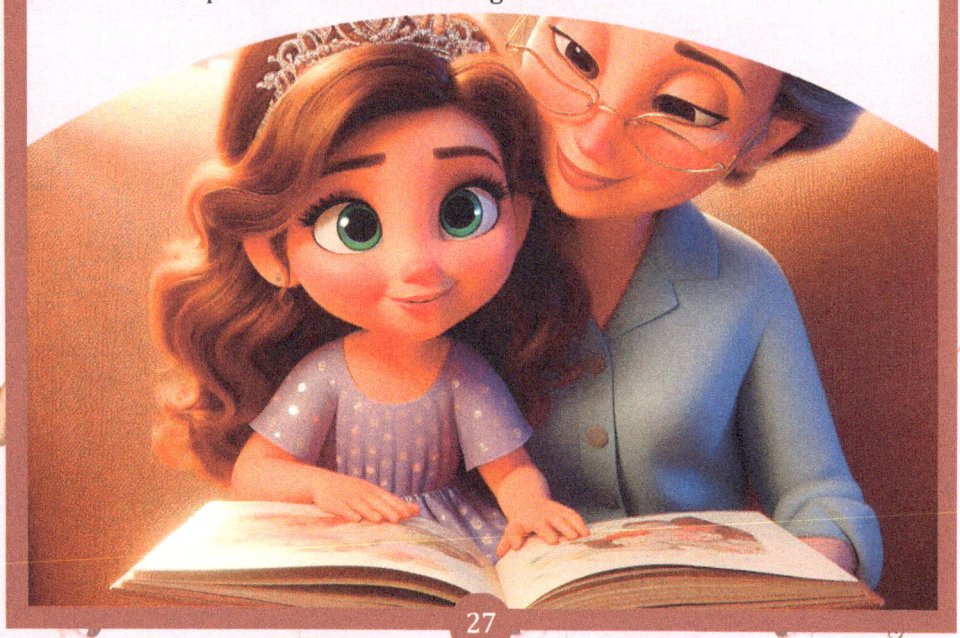

28

Coronation Dream - When Queen Victoria was just nine years old, she had a very special and vivid dream that she would remember for the rest of her life. In this dream, Victoria saw herself dressed in a long, beautiful robe, just like the ones kings and queens wear. On her head, she wore a crown, which is a symbol of being a ruler.

In the dream, Victoria was standing in a grand church, and the church was filled with many people. They were all there to see her and to be part of something very important. Even though it was just a dream, it felt very real to Victoria, and it made her feel like she was already a queen.

This dream was more than just a random thought in her sleep; it was a glimpse of what her future might look like. Even though she was still a young girl, this dream made Victoria feel a strong connection to her future role as queen. It was almost like the dream was reminding her of the big responsibility she would have one day.

After having this dream, Victoria couldn't forget it. It made her think even more about what it would mean to be a queen and how important it was to be prepared for that role. This dream helped her understand that being a queen wasn't just about wearing fancy clothes and a crown; it was about being a leader and doing her best for her country. So, even though Victoria was only nine years old, this coronation dream made her feel more aware of her destiny and the important path that lay ahead of her. It gave her a sense of purpose and reinforced her commitment to be the best queen she could be.

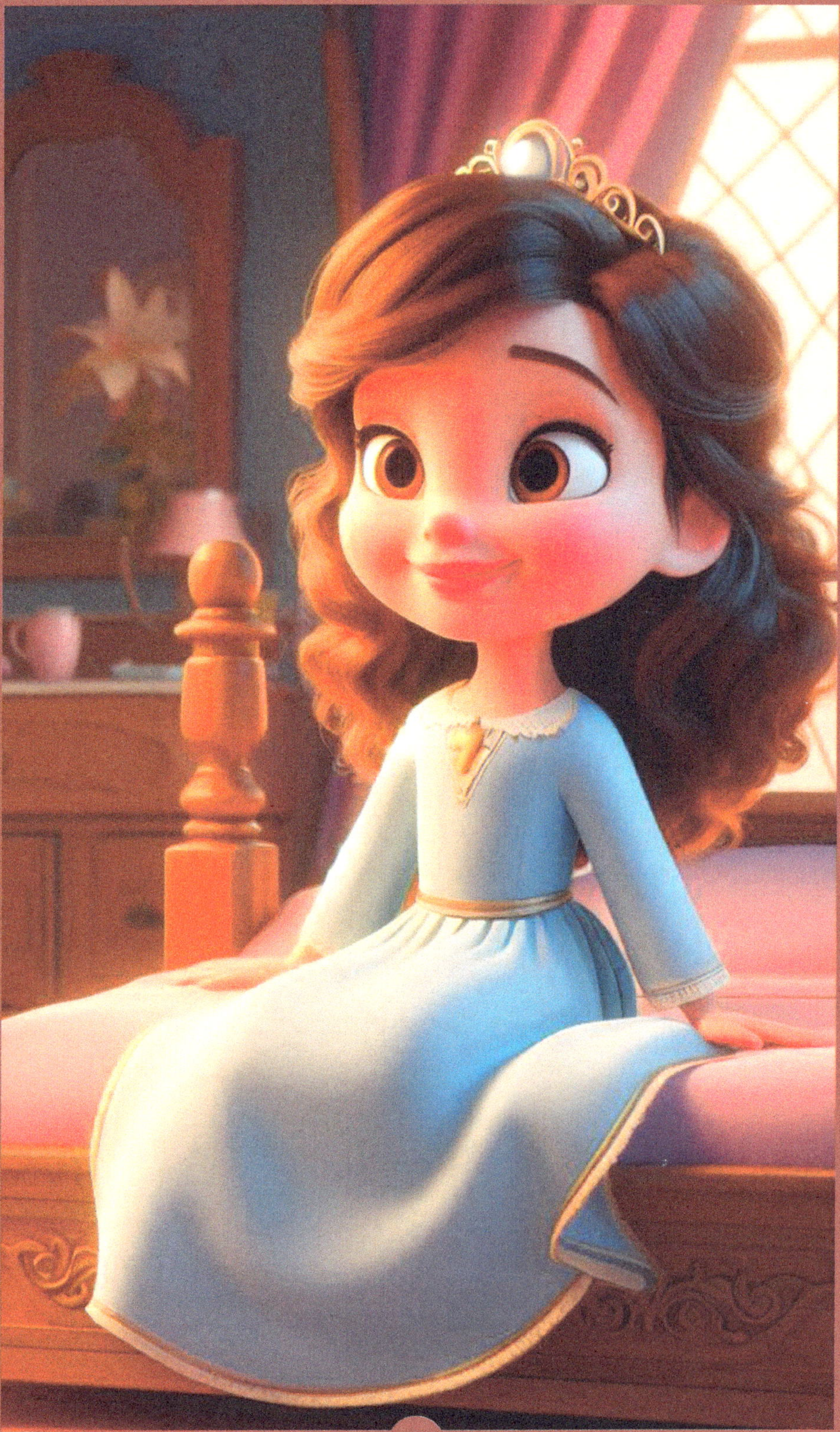

No Surname - When Queen Victoria was growing up, she didn't have a surname like most people do today. A surname is a last name that families use to identify themselves, such as "Smith" or "Johnson." Instead, Victoria was known by her title and the name of her family. Since Victoria was born before the royal family started using the name "Windsor," which they began using during World War I in 1917, she didn't have a last name at all. The royal family used the name "Windsor" to show a new, more British identity, but Victoria lived long before this change. As a child, Victoria was simply known as "Victoria of Kent." This name came from her father's title, the Duke of Kent, which was part of the royal family's name. "Kent" was used to show which part of the royal family she belonged to. Even though she didn't have a surname like most people, "Victoria of Kent" was a special name that marked her place in the royal family. So, even without a last name, Victoria was always recognized as a member of the royal family, and her name reflected her important position as a princess in the House of Kent.

The Day She Became Queen

"Do not give way to evil but combat it with good."
Queen Victoria

One quiet night, while most people were fast asleep, a young girl named Victoria was dreaming peacefully in her bed. She was just 18 years old and still lived in Kensington Palace with her mother. Her room was cozy, with soft curtains and a warm blanket that kept her snug as she slept.

It was the early morning of June 20, 1837. The sun had not yet risen, and the palace was still and silent. Suddenly, there was a knock on Victoria's door. She opened her eyes, surprised to hear a sound so early in the morning. Her governess, Baroness Lehzen, came in with a serious look on her face.

"Victoria, my dear, you must wake up," she said gently.

Victoria sat up in bed, rubbing her eyes. "What's happening?" she asked, feeling a little nervous.

Baroness Lehzen took a deep breath and spoke softly, "Your uncle, King William, has passed away during the night. This means, Victoria, that you are now the Queen of England."

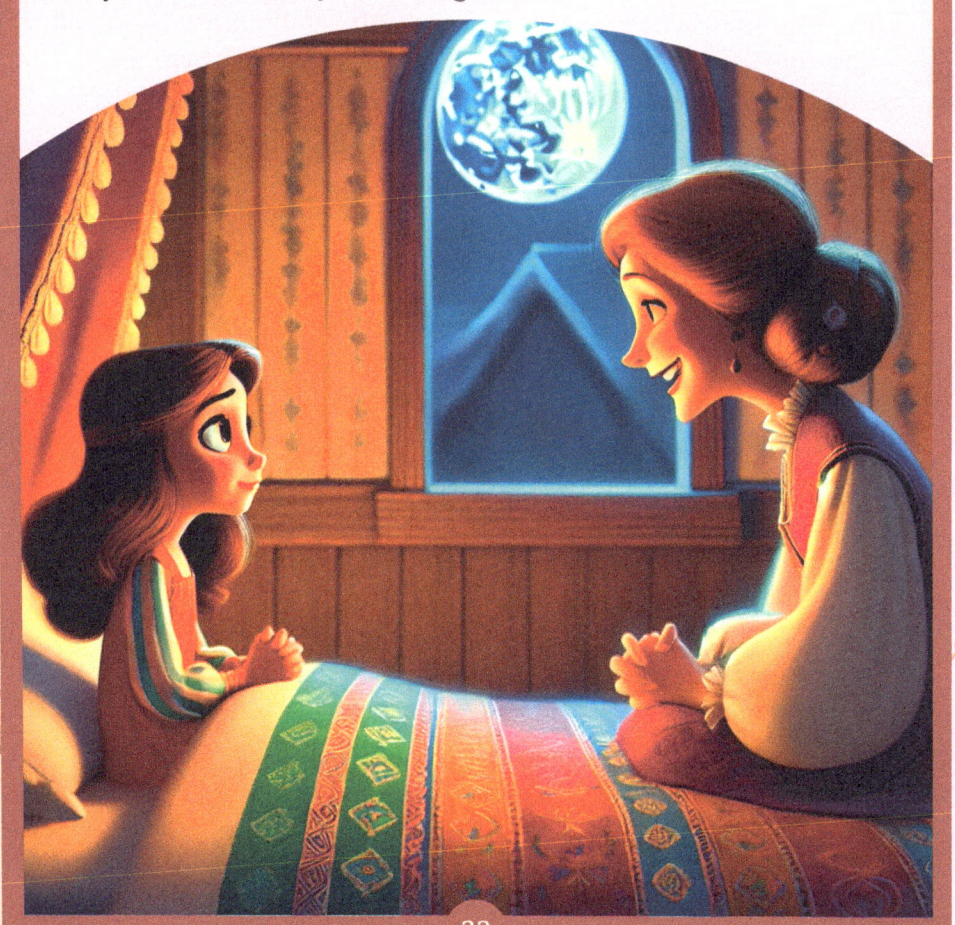

Victoria felt a shiver run down her spine. She was the Queen? It was a moment she had known would come someday, but she never imagined it would be so soon. The thought of it made her heart race. She was no longer just Princess Victoria; she was now Queen Victoria, the ruler of an entire country.

As she got out of bed and dressed, Victoria's mind was filled with a mix of emotions. She felt a great sense of responsibility, knowing that so many people would now look to her for guidance. But she also felt a flicker of excitement. This was the beginning of a new chapter in her life, a chapter where she could make a difference and help her people.

Later that morning, in a small, elegant room filled with sunlight, Victoria held her first meeting as Queen. She sat in a chair that seemed too big for her, with important ministers and advisors gathered around. They all bowed to her, and she knew that from this moment on, she had to be strong and wise, just like the queens she had read about in her books.

The days that followed were full of preparations for a grand event—the Coronation. This was the special ceremony where Victoria would officially be crowned as Queen. The whole country was buzzing with excitement, and people traveled from far and wide to see their new young queen.

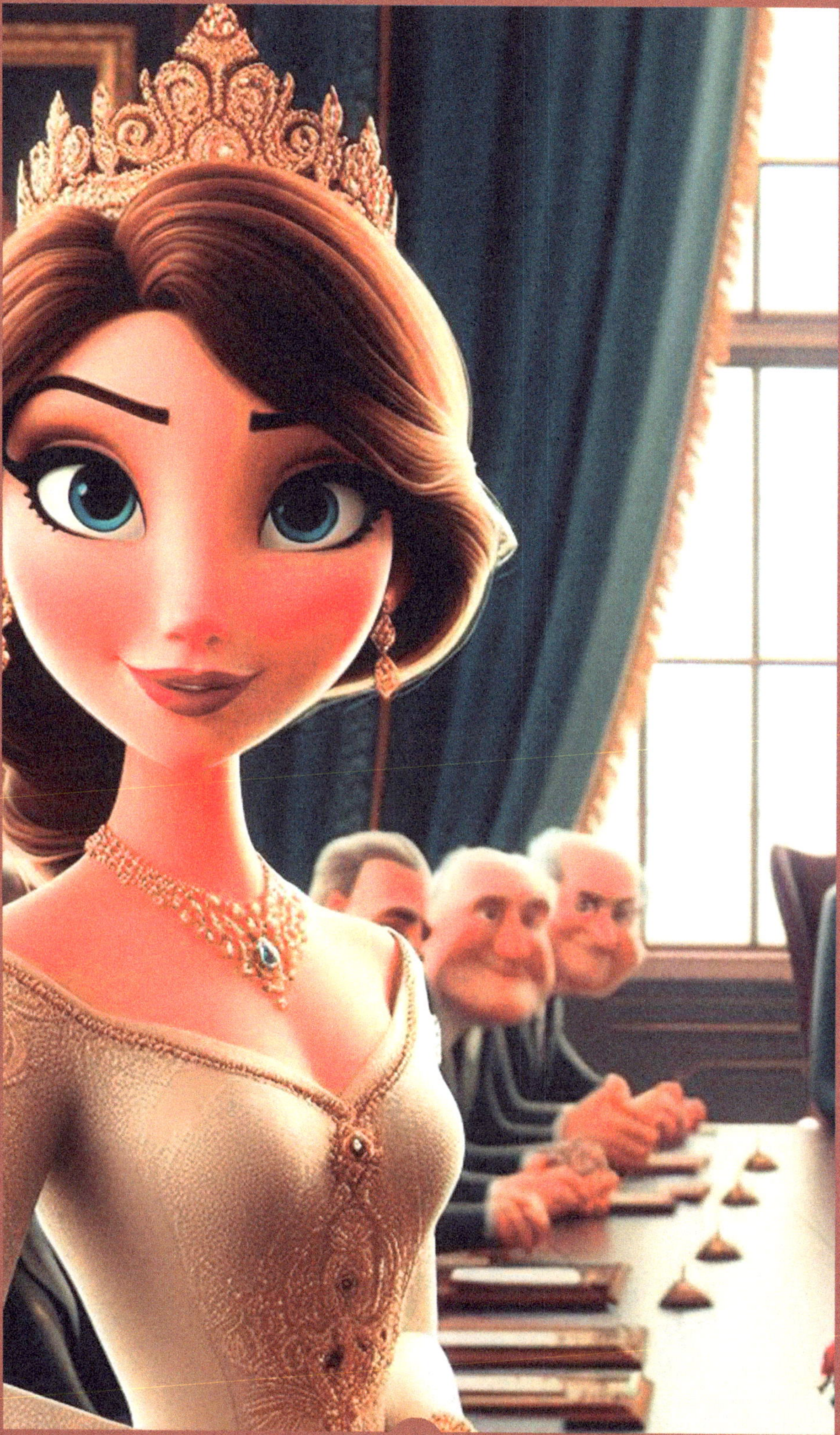

On the day of the Coronation, Victoria wore a beautiful white dress with a long train that flowed behind her like a river of silk. Her heart fluttered as she walked down the long aisle of Westminster Abbey, the grand church where the ceremony was held. The walls were lined with colorful banners, and the sound of music filled the air.

As she reached the front of the Abbey, Victoria knelt down. The Archbishop, a wise and gentle man, placed a glittering crown on her head. It was heavy, but Victoria held her head high. In that moment, she felt the weight of her new role, but she also felt a deep sense of pride. She was no longer just a young girl; she was now Queen Victoria, the leader of a great nation.

The crowds outside cheered loudly as the new queen stepped out of the Abbey. Thousands of people had gathered to see her, waving flags and shouting her name. Victoria smiled and waved back, feeling a connection to each and every one of them. She knew they were counting on her, and she promised herself that she would be the best queen she could be.

As she rode back to the palace in a golden carriage, Victoria looked out at the faces of her people. She was still the same girl who loved books, gardens, and her dolls. But now, she had a new purpose, a new role to play. And as she looked up at the sky, she knew deep in her heart that she was ready for the adventure ahead. From that day forward, Victoria was not just a princess in a palace—she was the Queen of England, and her journey had only just begun.

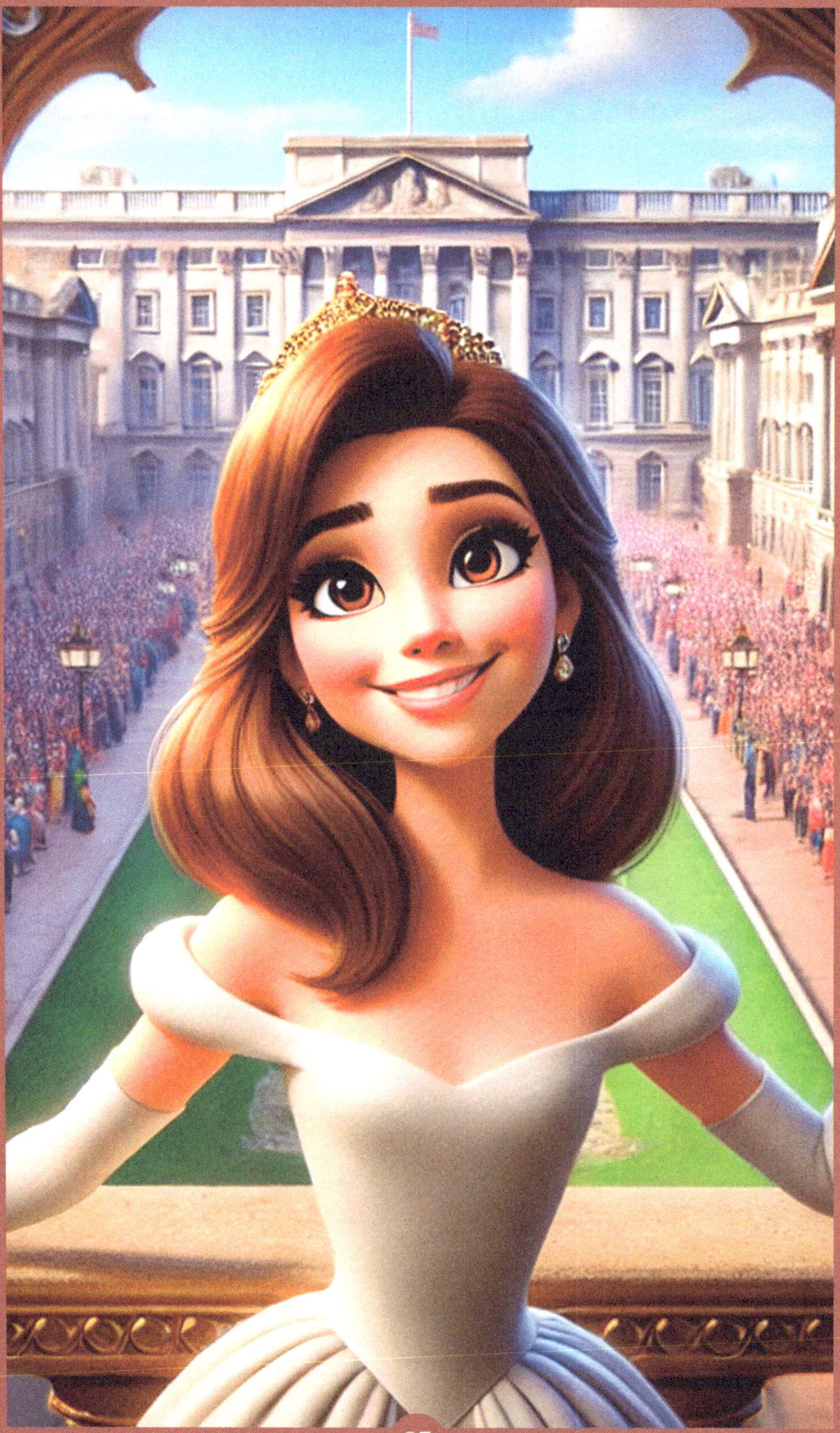

Fascinating Facts about Queen Victoria's Coronation:

A Lavish Event - Queen Victoria's coronation ceremony was a big, fancy event, like a super special party to celebrate her becoming queen. The place where it all happened was Westminster Abbey, a grand church in London.

To make everything look amazing, the Abbey was decorated with thousands of candles that made the place glow beautifully. There were also lots of colorful flowers everywhere, adding to the cheerful and grand feeling of the ceremony.

Many important people came to the ceremony. These included royalty from other countries, important leaders, and special guests. They all came to watch and celebrate with Victoria as she started her new role as queen. Overall, the ceremony was not just about making Victoria queen; it was also a grand and memorable celebration filled with beautiful decorations and important guests.

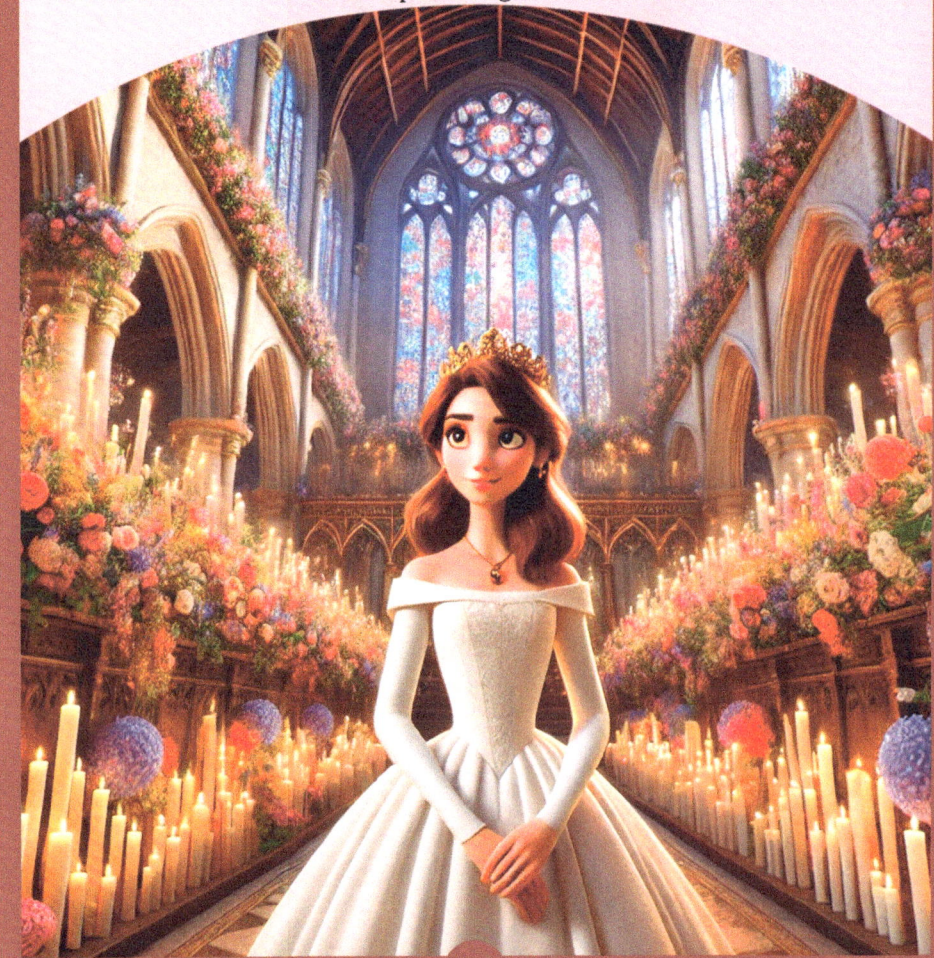

Coronation Robes - For her coronation, Queen Victoria wore some truly spectacular clothes. She put on a set of special robes that were made from very rich and luxurious fabrics. These fabrics were soft and shiny, making her look like a real queen. Her coronation dress was extra special because it was decorated with sparkling gold and shiny diamonds. This made the dress look very elegant and important. The gold and diamonds helped show that Victoria was now the queen and that she had a lot of power. Victoria also wore a traditional crown during the ceremony. This crown was a very special part of the coronation. It was designed to show her royal status and to make her look like the queen she was becoming. The robes and the crown were not just beautiful; they were also quite heavy. They were made to be grand and impressive, but they also reminded everyone of the big responsibilities that came with being a queen. So, while Victoria looked magnificent in her robes and crown, they also showed how important and serious her new role was.

The Coronation Oath - During Queen Victoria's coronation ceremony, she took something very important called the Coronation Oath. This was a special promise she made to her country and its people.

In the Coronation Oath, Victoria promised to follow all the laws and rules of the land. This means she agreed to make sure that everyone, including herself, followed the rules that kept the country running smoothly. She also promised to do what was right and to be fair to everyone, which means she would govern with justice and make decisions that were best for her people.

Taking the Coronation Oath was a key part of becoming queen. It wasn't just a formality; it was a serious and important promise that showed Victoria's dedication to her new role. By taking this oath, she was showing that she understood her big responsibility to lead the country well and to serve her people with honor and fairness.

Public and Private - During Queen Victoria's coronation, there were both big public celebrations and quiet private moments.

Public Spectacle: The coronation was a grand event that everyone could see. There were lots of guests, beautiful decorations, and a lot of excitement. People came from all over to watch Victoria be crowned and to celebrate with her. It was a big, joyful occasion that showed how important and special her new role as queen was.

Private Moments: After the big, public part of the ceremony was over, Victoria had some time alone. This was a quiet and private part of the coronation where she went off by herself to pray and think about her new responsibilities. This time was very important because it allowed her to reflect on the serious promises she had made and to prepare herself for the duties of being queen.

So, while everyone enjoyed the grand and festive parts of the coronation, Victoria also had moments of peace and contemplation to get ready for her important role as the ruler of her country.

Fainting Incident - During Queen Victoria's coronation, something dramatic happened that made everyone in the room quite worried. While the ceremony was going on, Victoria suddenly fainted. This means she lost consciousness and fell to the ground, which was a surprising and scary moment for everyone there.

When she fainted, the room was filled with concern. People were worried about her and wanted to make sure she was okay. Luckily, Victoria quickly woke up and felt better. She recovered soon after, and the ceremony was able to continue without too much delay.

Even though it was a scary moment, Victoria's quick recovery allowed the important event to go on as planned. The ceremony was a big and significant occasion, and Victoria's return to her place helped ensure that everything ended up being just as special as it was meant to be.

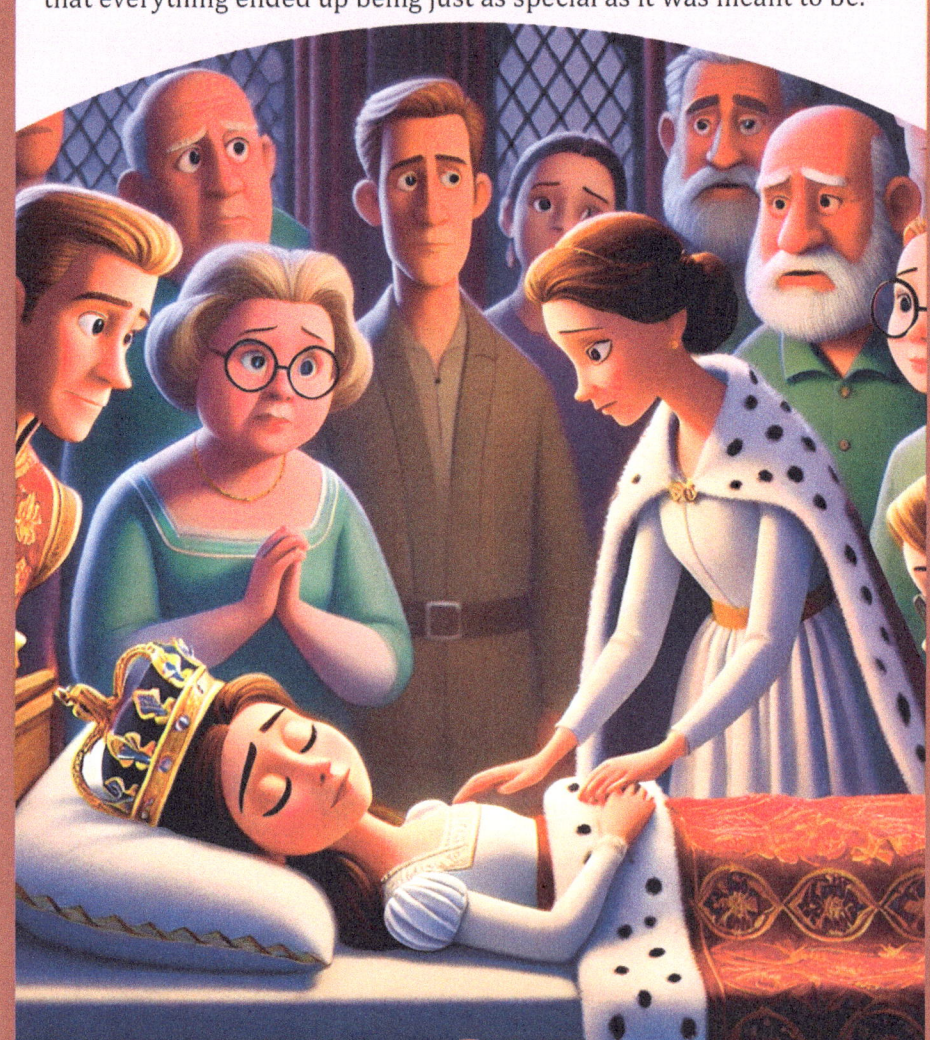

First to See the Ceremony - Queen Victoria was the first monarch to have a large painting made of her own coronation ceremony. This was a big deal because no king or queen before her had ever seen such a detailed and grand picture of their special day.

The artist, George Hayter, was chosen to create this painting. He did a wonderful job capturing the beauty and importance of the ceremony. The painting showed all the key moments of the coronation, with Victoria in her beautiful robes and crown, surrounded by all the important people who attended the event.

After the painting was finished, it was put on display so that everyone could see it. People from all over could look at the painting and feel like they were part of the ceremony, even if they hadn't been there in person. This made Victoria's coronation even more special because it was preserved in a way that future generations could admire and remember.

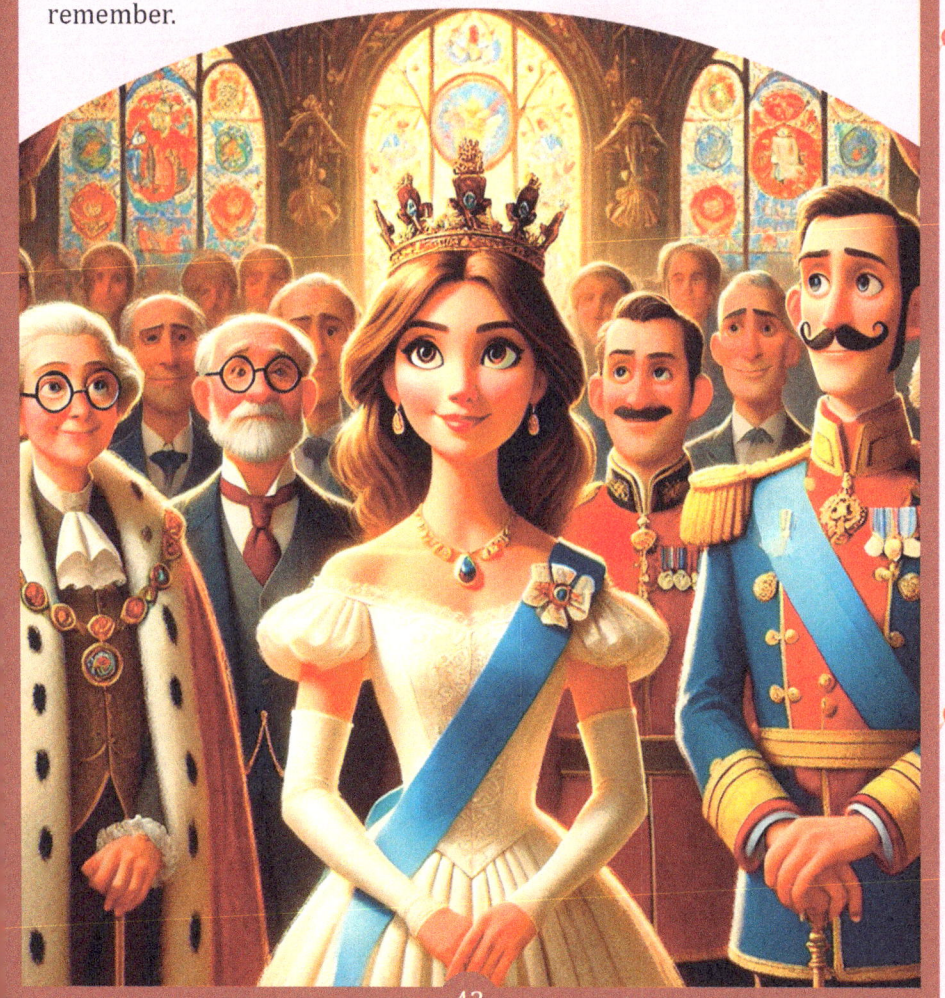

A Young Queen's First Decisions

"Nothing will turn me from my purpose."
Queen Victoria

Now that Victoria was Queen, she had many important decisions to make. Though she was still young, just 18 years old, she was determined to be a good and wise ruler for her people. She knew that being Queen wasn't just about wearing a crown and attending fancy events. It was about making choices that would help her country and the people who lived there. One of the first big decisions Victoria made was about where she would live. Up until now, she had always lived at Kensington Palace with her mother. But now that she was Queen, she needed a place of her own where she could rule the country and meet with important people. After thinking carefully, Victoria decided that she would move to Buckingham Palace, a grand and beautiful palace in the heart of London. Buckingham Palace was larger and grander than Kensington Palace, with big, sparkling chandeliers, tall windows, and wide gardens full of colorful flowers. Victoria loved it at once. She chose it as her new home because she felt it was the perfect place to start her life as a queen. The move to Buckingham Palace marked the beginning of a new chapter in her life, one filled with both challenges and exciting opportunities.

As Victoria settled into her new home, she began to learn more about the responsibilities of being Queen. She worked closely with her advisors, who were older and more experienced, but she quickly realized that she couldn't rely on them for everything. Victoria was smart and thoughtful, and she knew that some decisions had to come from her own heart and mind. One day, Victoria was asked to make an important decision about a new law. Her advisors gave her lots of advice, each with their own ideas about what should be done. They spoke with big words and serious faces, but Victoria listened carefully, taking in everything they said. After they were finished, she thought about it long and hard. She wanted to make sure that whatever she chose would be best for her people. Finally, Victoria spoke up. She had made her decision, and it was different from what some of her advisors had suggested. She explained her choice clearly, showing that she had considered all the options. Her advisors were surprised but impressed. Even though she was young, Victoria showed them that she had the wisdom and courage to make the right choices for her country.

Victoria's days were filled with many more decisions like this. She met with people from all over the country, listened to their needs, and made choices that would help them. She cared deeply about her people and wanted to do everything she could to make their lives better. Even when the decisions were difficult, Victoria always put her people first.

She quickly became known as a queen who was more than just a figurehead. She was a leader who cared, who thought carefully about every decision she made, and who was dedicated to making her country a better place. Victoria took her role seriously, but she also loved it. She was proud to be Queen, and every day she worked hard to be the best ruler she could be.

As time passed, Victoria's confidence grew. She learned to trust her own judgment and to make decisions that were best for her people, even when they were tough. And with every choice she made, she showed the world that she was not just a young girl wearing a crown—she was a true queen, ready to lead her country into a bright and hopeful future.

Victoria's reign was only just beginning, but already she was proving herself to be a strong and capable leader. With Buckingham Palace as her home and her heart full of determination, Queen Victoria was ready to face whatever challenges lay ahead. And she knew that as long as she stayed true to herself and her people, she could make a difference in the world.

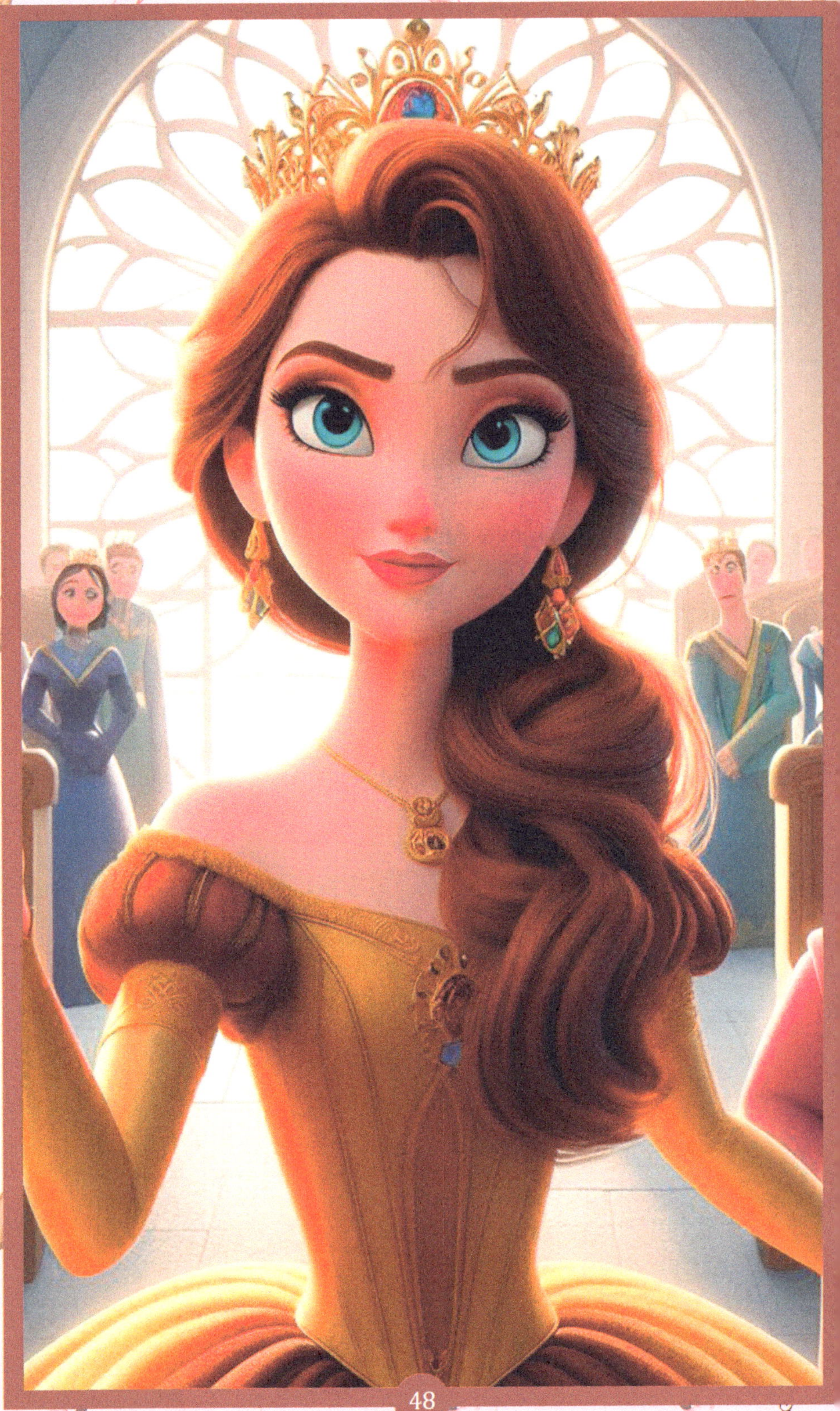

Fascinating Facts about Queen Victoria:

The Longest Reign (Until Recently) - Queen Victoria was queen for a very long time—63 years! She started ruling in 1837 when she was just 18 years old, and she continued to be queen until she passed away in 1901. That's a lot of years to be in charge! During those 63 years, many things changed and got better in Britain. There were new inventions, better ways of doing things, and important laws that helped people. Queen Victoria saw all of these changes happen and was a big part of them. For a long time, Queen Victoria was the longest-reigning monarch, which means she ruled longer than any other king or queen before her. But much later, her great-great-granddaughter, Queen Elizabeth II, became queen and ruled for even longer than Victoria did! So, Queen Victoria held the record for a long time, but then Queen Elizabeth II took over that title. Queen Victoria's long time as queen was very important because she helped guide her country through so many changes, making sure Britain grew and improved during her reign.

Supporting Social Reforms - Queen Victoria cared a lot about making life better for her people, so she supported many important changes, called social reforms. These changes helped improve things like education, health, and the way people worked.

Education: Victoria believed that everyone should have the chance to go to school and learn. During her time as queen, more schools were built, and more children were able to get an education. This helped kids learn to read, write, and gain important skills they would need when they grew up.

Health: Victoria was also interested in making sure people were healthy. During her reign, new hospitals were built, and better medical care became available. This helped people live longer, healthier lives.

Working Conditions: During Victoria's time, many people worked in factories, and the conditions were often very hard and unsafe, especially for children. Victoria supported new laws that made working conditions safer and fairer. These laws protected workers, making sure they weren't forced to work too many hours and that children were no longer allowed to do dangerous jobs.

Thanks to Queen Victoria's support for these social reforms, life became much better and safer for many people in Britain. She helped create a country where people could live healthier lives, learn new things, and work in safer places.

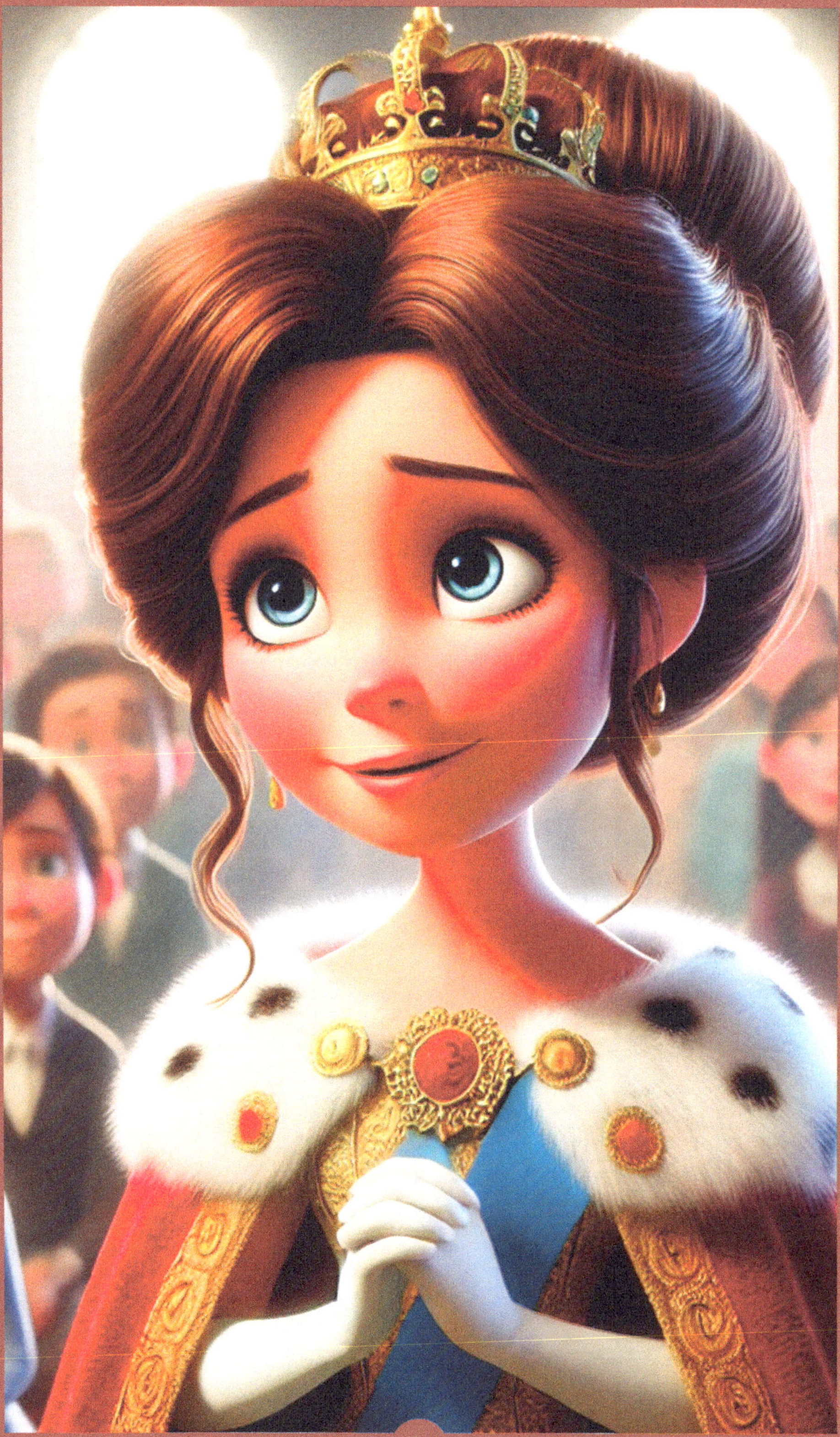

Expanding the British Empire - During Queen Victoria's time as queen, the British Empire became the biggest in the world. This means that Britain gained control over many different countries and territories all around the globe. Because the British Empire was so large and spread across so many time zones, there was always some part of it where the sun was shining. That's why people started saying, "The sun never sets on the British Empire." It was a way of showing just how vast and powerful the empire had become. These new territories included places in Africa, Asia, the Americas, and the Pacific. Britain's influence reached far and wide, and Queen Victoria was seen as the ruler of not just Britain, but many other parts of the world as well. While the expansion of the empire made Britain very powerful and wealthy, it also had a big impact on the people living in the countries that became part of the empire. Some of these effects were good, like the introduction of new technologies and education, but there were also challenges and difficulties for the people in those lands.Queen Victoria's rule was a time when Britain's power spread across the world, making the British Empire the largest and most influential empire in history.

Promoting Education - Queen Victoria really believed that education was important for everyone. During her time as queen, she worked to make sure that more children had the chance to go to school and learn. Before Victoria's reign, not all kids could go to school, especially if their families didn't have much money. But Victoria supported changes that made schools more available to all children, no matter where they came from or how much money their families had. This meant that more boys and girls could go to school, learn to read and write, and get a good education. Because more children were able to go to school, they learned important skills that helped them as they grew up. Being able to read and write opened up new opportunities for them, like better jobs and a brighter future. It also helped the whole country because when more people are educated, they can contribute more to society, come up with new ideas, and help their country grow and improve. Thanks to Queen Victoria's support for education, Britain became a place where learning was valued, and more people had the chance to succeed. This focus on education helped the country move forward and become stronger.

Popularizing Christmas Traditions - Queen Victoria and her husband, Prince Albert, played a big role in making Christmas traditions popular that we still enjoy today. One of the things they helped make famous was decorating Christmas trees. Before Victoria and Albert, Christmas trees were not very common in Britain. But Prince Albert, who was from Germany, brought this lovely tradition with him. He and Victoria decorated their own Christmas tree with candles, tinsel, and ornaments. It looked so beautiful and festive that people everywhere started copying them. They also liked to celebrate Christmas with special treats and family gatherings, and they made these customs even more popular. Because Victoria and Albert enjoyed these traditions so much, other families began to do the same. Thanks to them, decorating Christmas trees became a favorite part of the holiday for many people. Every year, families all over the world now put up their own Christmas trees and decorate them with lights, ornaments, and star-toppers, just like Victoria and Albert did. So, Victoria and Prince Albert's love for Christmas traditions made the holiday even more special for everyone, helping to create some of the festive customs we still cherish today.

Modernizing the Monarchy - Queen Victoria played a big part in changing the way people saw the British monarchy. Before her time, the royal family was often seen as distant and separate from everyday life. But Victoria worked hard to make the monarchy feel closer and more connected to the people.

Victoria showed that the royal family could be more involved in the lives of ordinary people. She made sure that the royal family wasn't just a group of people living far away and only seen at big events. Instead, she tried to be a part of everyday life, making the monarchy feel more personal and approachable. Victoria started making more public appearances and attending events where she could meet and interact with everyday people. This helped people feel like they knew their queen and made the monarchy feel more like a part of their lives. Victoria also shared more about her family life. She made sure that people saw her as a mother and wife, not just a queen. This made her more relatable and showed that she understood what ordinary families went through.

By being involved in everyday events and showing her connection to the people, Victoria became a symbol of national pride. People began to see the royal family as a symbol of their country and its values, which made them feel proud and united. Through her actions and choices, Queen Victoria helped modernize the monarchy and made it a more meaningful and comforting presence in the lives of ordinary people. Her efforts showed that being a royal could be about more than just ruling—it could be about connecting with the people and being a part of their everyday lives.

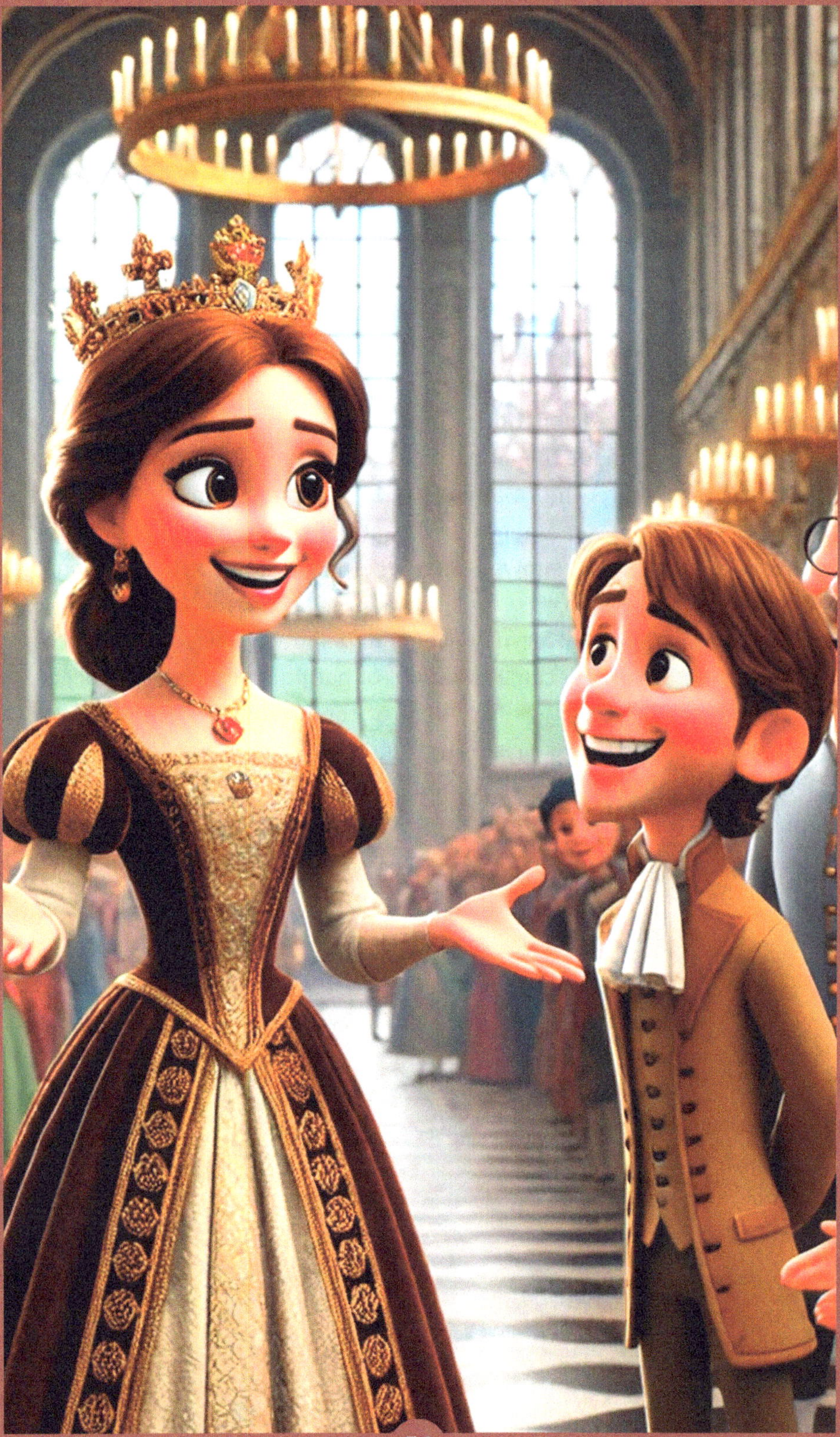

A Love Story - Victoria and Albert

"A marriage is no amusement but a solemn act, and generally a sad one."
Queen Victoria

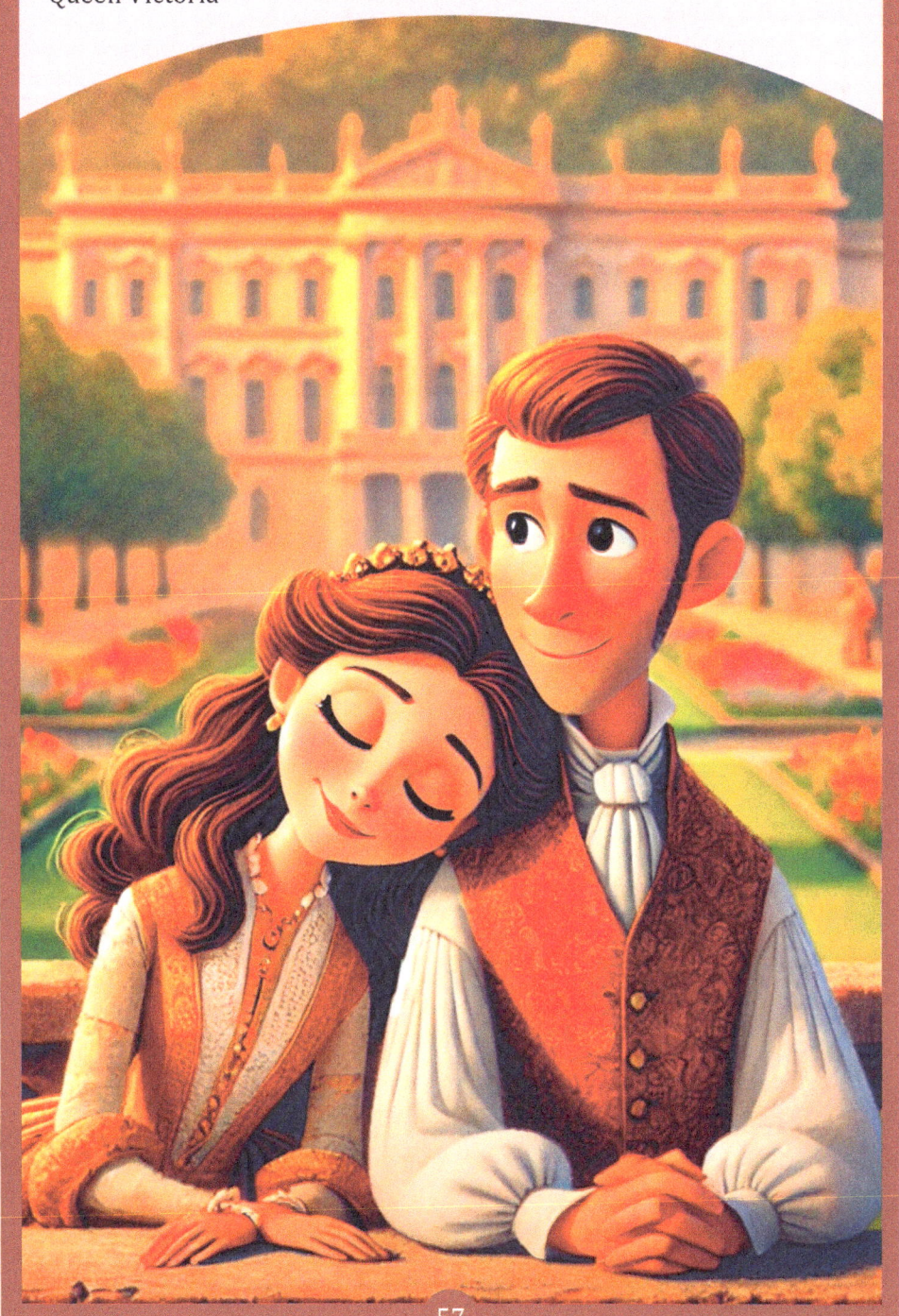

As Queen Victoria settled into her role as the ruler of England, she worked hard every day. But even queens need love and companionship, and for Victoria, that special person was just around the corner. This is the story of how Queen Victoria met the love of her life, Prince Albert.

Victoria had known Prince Albert of Saxe-Coburg and Gotha for many years. Albert was her cousin, and they had first met when they were both young. At that time, they were just children, and while they liked each other, they didn't think much about the future. But as they grew older, something magical began to happen.

One day, when Victoria was 20 years old, Prince Albert came to visit her at Buckingham Palace. He had grown into a handsome and kind young man, with a warm smile and gentle eyes. Victoria was instantly taken by his charm and grace. As they spent time together, walking through the palace gardens and talking about their hopes and dreams, Victoria realized that she felt something special for Albert—something she had never felt before.

Albert, too, was enchanted by Victoria. He admired her strength and intelligence, and he could see that beneath her crown and royal duties, she was a kind and caring person. They both knew that what they felt was love, and soon, they couldn't imagine life without each other.

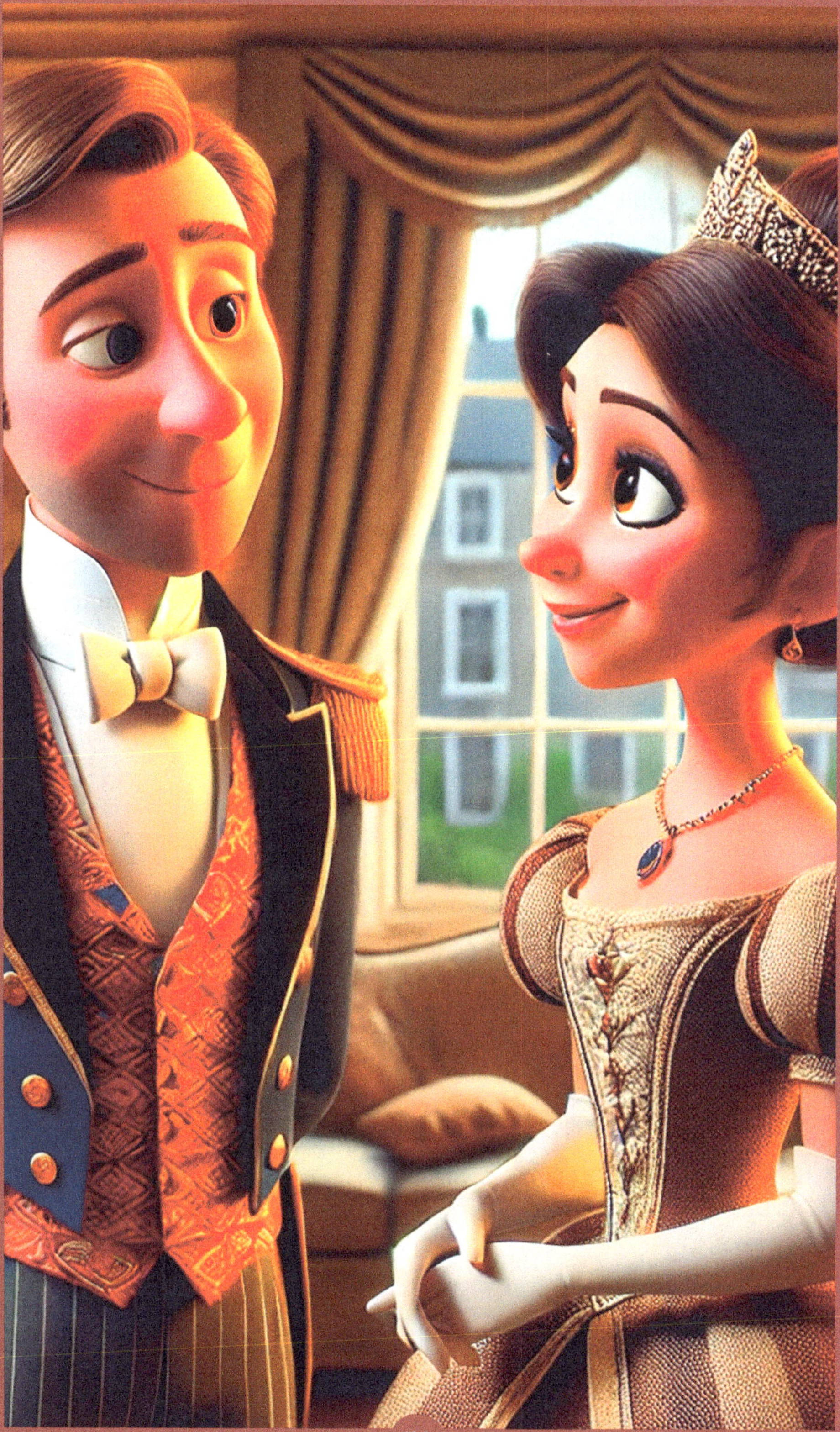

Not long after, Albert proposed to Victoria, and she joyfully accepted. She was so happy that she couldn't wait to tell everyone the good news! They planned a beautiful wedding, and on a chilly day in February 1840, Victoria and Albert were married in a grand ceremony at the Chapel Royal in St. James's Palace. Victoria wore a stunning white dress, which was very special because back then, brides usually wore silver or gold. But Victoria wanted to start a new tradition, and her white gown became the symbol of purity and love. As she walked down the aisle, her heart was full of joy. She knew she had found her true partner in life, someone who would stand by her side through all the challenges of being a queen. After their wedding, Victoria and Albert became inseparable. They were not just husband and wife; they were best friends and partners in everything they did. They loved spending time together, whether it was taking walks in the gardens, playing music, or working on important projects for their country. Albert was not just a prince—he was Victoria's most trusted advisor, and they often worked side by side on issues that mattered to them both.

One of their greatest passions was improving the lives of their people. Together, they supported many projects that helped schools, hospitals, and the arts. Albert encouraged Victoria to continue her education and always be curious about the world. They shared a love for learning, and together, they made England a better place.

Victoria and Albert's love was deep and true. They were a team, and they faced every challenge together, whether it was running the country or raising their nine children. Yes, they had a big family, and their children were raised with the same love and care that Victoria and Albert had for each other.

Their love story became famous all over the world, and people admired how close they were. Even though Victoria was a queen and had many responsibilities, she always made time for Albert, and he always supported her. They were a perfect match, and their love for each other only grew stronger with time.

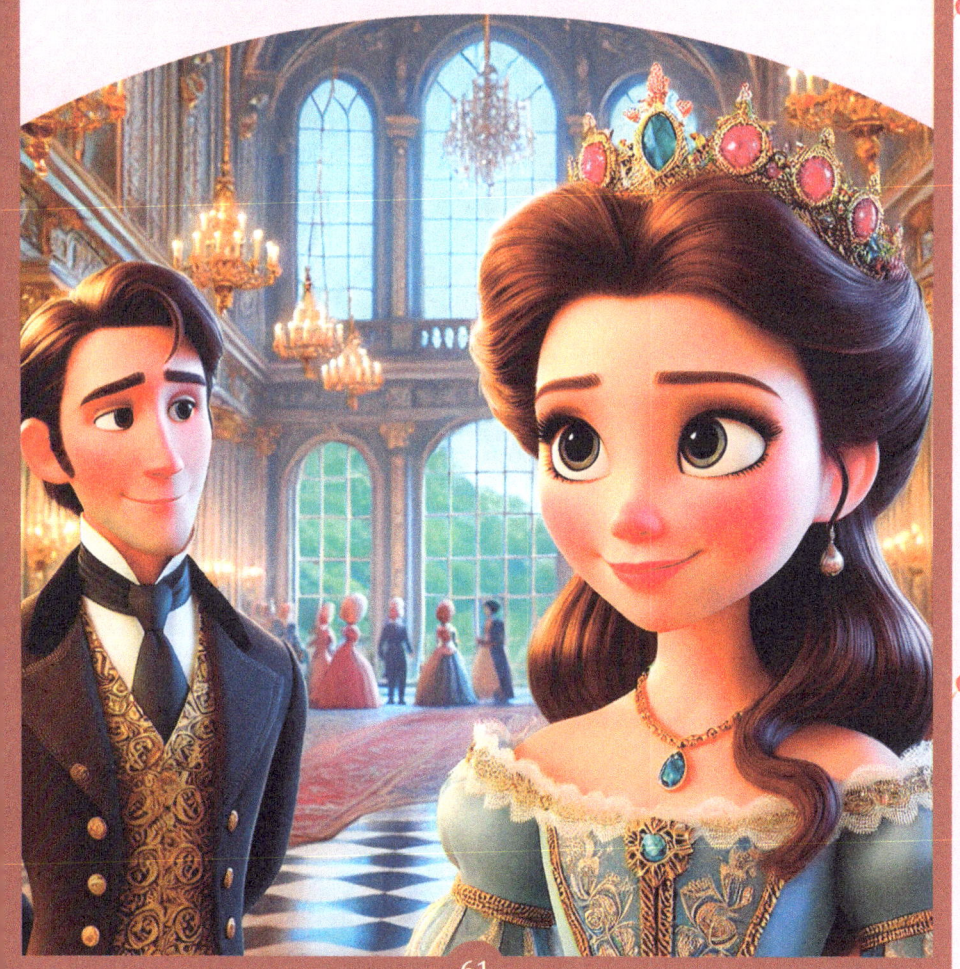

Victoria often said that marrying Albert was the happiest day of her life, and she treasured every moment they spent together. They showed the world that love is not just about grand gestures or fairy tales—it's about partnership, respect, and always being there for each other.

As the years went by, Victoria and Albert continued to build a life full of love, happiness, and hard work. Their story is one that reminds us all of the power of true love and how it can make even the hardest days a little bit brighter.

And so, in the grand halls of Buckingham Palace, and in the hearts of the people, the love story of Queen Victoria and Prince Albert became a legend—a beautiful tale of a queen and her prince who lived happily ever after.

Fascinating Facts about Queen Victoria's Marriage and Children:

Love at First Sight - Queen Victoria's love story with Prince Albert is a very special one.

When Victoria was just 16 years old, she met Prince Albert, who was her first cousin. Even though they were related, it was very common for royals to marry within the family during that time. As soon as Victoria met Albert, she felt something very special for him. She quickly fell in love with him because he was kind, smart, and handsome.

A few years later, when Victoria was 20 years old, they got married on February 10, 1840. In those days, many royal marriages were arranged for political reasons, not because of love. But Victoria and Albert's marriage was different. They married because they truly loved each other, which was unusual for royals at that time.

Since Victoria was the queen, it was her job to propose to Albert. In those days, a man usually asked a woman to marry him, but because Victoria was the queen, she had to ask Albert herself. She was so happy when he said yes!

Their love for each other was deep and real, and they had a very happy marriage. Victoria adored Albert and always felt lucky to have him as her husband.

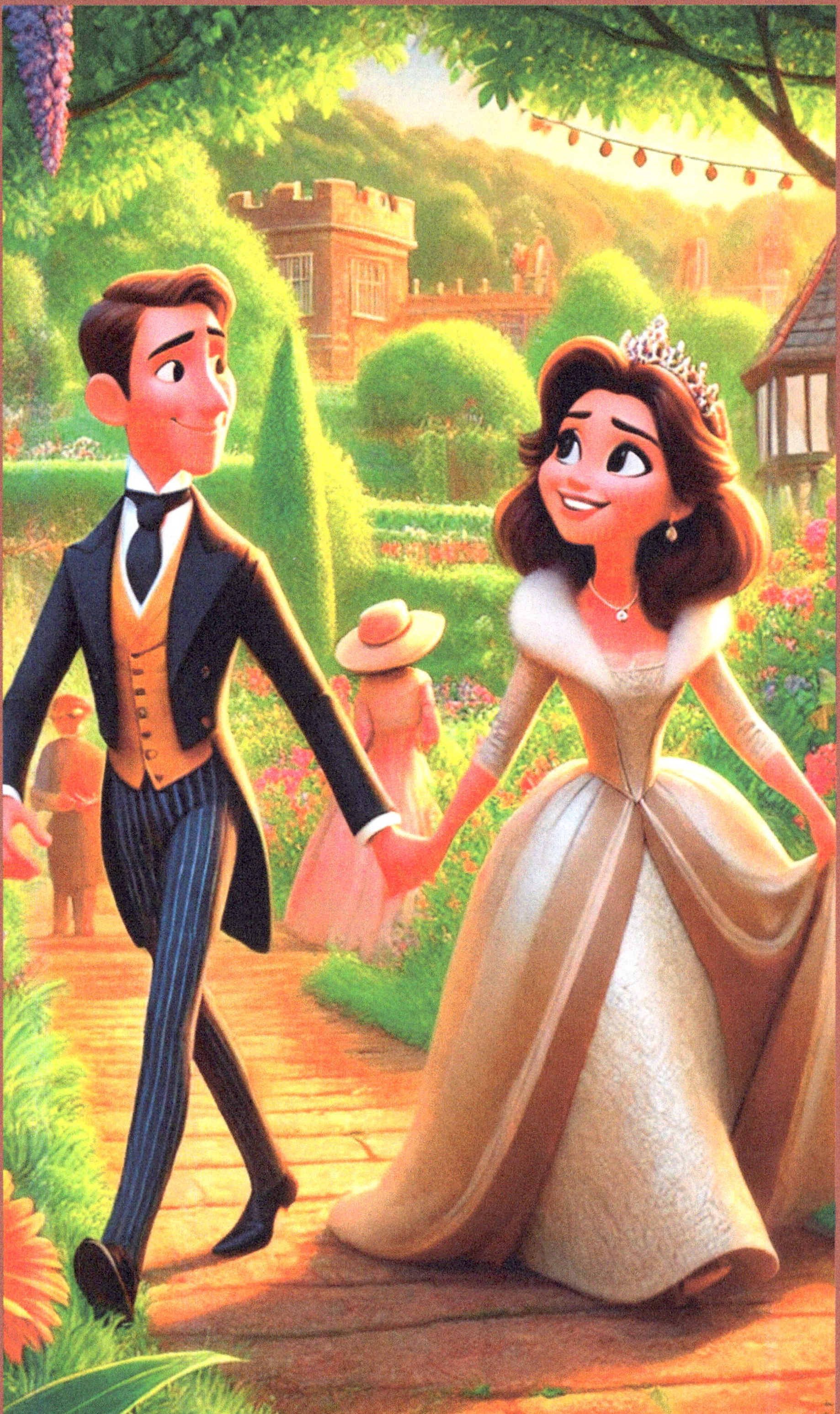

A Happy Marriage - Queen Victoria and Prince Albert had a very close and happy marriage. They loved each other very much and enjoyed spending time together. They didn't just share their lives as husband and wife; they also worked on many projects together and made important decisions about the country. One of the things that made their marriage special was how much they helped and supported each other. Albert wasn't just Victoria's husband; he was also her best friend and advisor. Whenever Victoria had to make a big decision, she would talk to Albert, and he would give her advice. This made their bond even stronger. Victoria loved Albert so much that she often called him her "beloved," which is a very special word for someone you love deeply. They were very happy raising their nine children and creating a loving family. But their happiness didn't last forever. Sadly, Albert passed away when he was still young, and Victoria was heartbroken. She was so sad that she wore black clothes for the rest of her life to show how much she missed him. She mourned Albert for 40 years, which shows just how much she loved and cherished him. Even though he was gone, she kept him in her heart forever.

Nine Children - Victoria and Albert had nine children—five daughters and four sons. Their names were:

Victoria (Vicky) - She married the German Emperor Frederick III and became the mother of Kaiser Wilhelm II.

Albert Edward (Bertie) - He became King Edward VII after Victoria's death.

Alice - She married Louis IV, Grand Duke of Hesse, and her daughter Alix became the last Empress of Russia.

Alfred - He became the Duke of Edinburgh and later the Duke of Saxe-Coburg and Gotha.

Helena - She married Prince Christian of Schleswig-Holstein and was involved in charity work.

Louise - She married John Campbell, the Duke of Argyll, and was a talented artist.

Arthur - He had a military career and served as Governor-General of Canada.

Leopold - He had hemophilia, a blood disorder, and died young at 30.

Beatrice - She was very close to Victoria and stayed with her mother until Victoria's death. She later married Prince Henry of Battenberg.

Royal Connections - Queen Victoria and Prince Albert had nine children, and as they grew up, many of them got married to princes and princesses from other countries in Europe. Because of this, Victoria and Albert's family became connected to many royal families across Europe. This is why they are often called the "grandparents of Europe."

When their children married into different royal families, it created strong ties between the countries. For example, one of their daughters, Victoria (known as Vicky), married the German Emperor, and their son Edward became King of England after Victoria. Another daughter, Alice, had children who became important royals in other countries, like Russia.

These marriages meant that the royal families of countries like Germany, Russia, and Spain were all related to Queen Victoria and Prince Albert. This is one of the reasons why so many kings, queens, princes, and princesses in Europe today are actually related to each other.

Because of these connections, Victoria and Albert's descendants are spread across many European countries, making them very important figures in European history. This family web is why Queen Victoria is sometimes called "the grandmother of Europe," and Prince Albert "the grandfather of Europe." Their family ties helped shape the relationships between countries for many years.

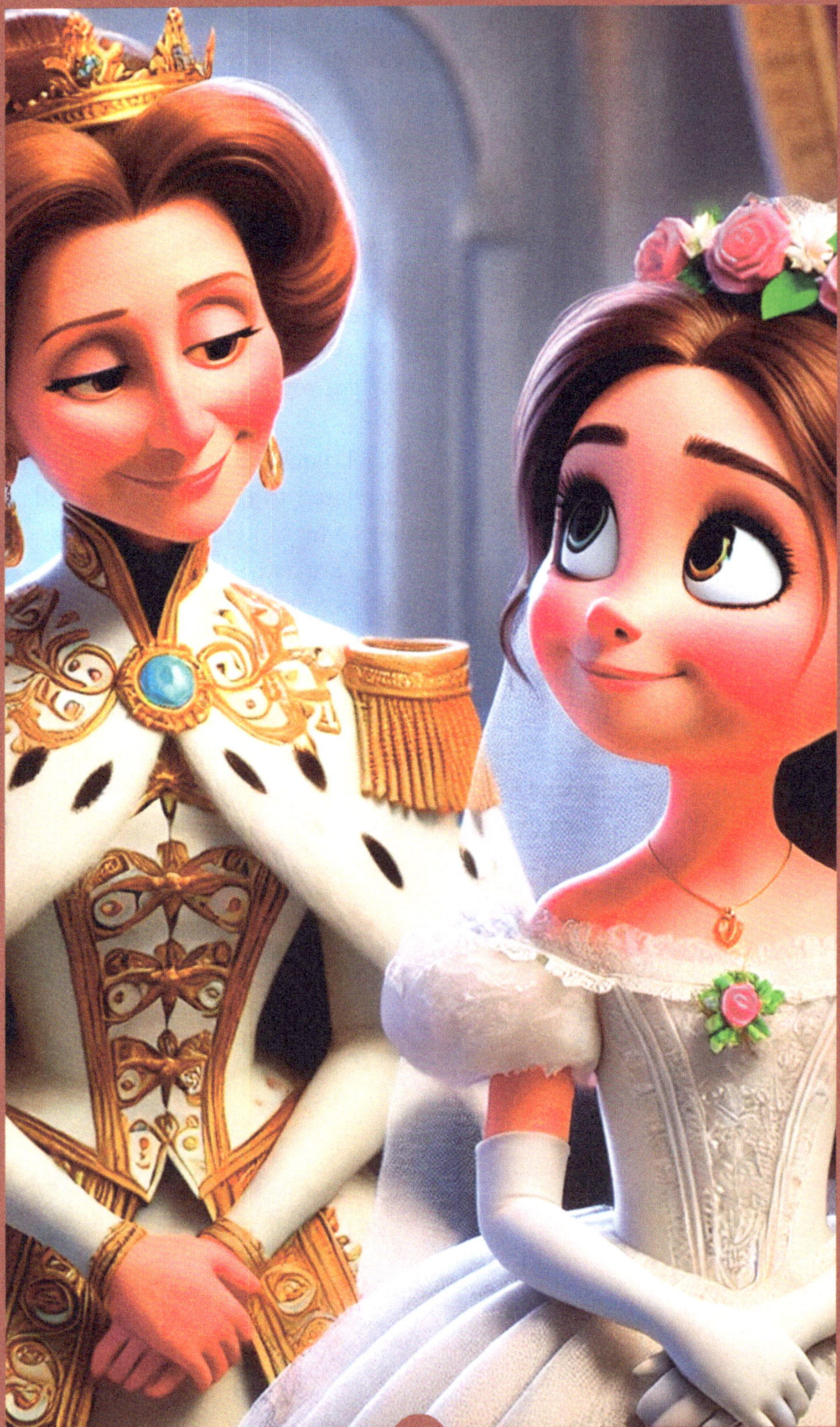

Family Life - Even though Queen Victoria had a lot of responsibilities as the queen, she was very involved in raising her children. She had nine children, and she cared about them deeply. Victoria could be strict at times, making sure her children behaved well and followed the rules. But she also loved them very much and wanted the best for them.

Prince Albert, Victoria's husband, was also very involved in their children's lives. He believed that education was very important, so he made sure that their children learned a lot, not just about school subjects like math and languages, but also about how to be responsible and kind. He wanted them to be ready for their future roles as members of the royal family. Victoria and Albert worked together to give their children a strong upbringing. They wanted their kids to grow up to be smart, caring, and prepared for the important duties they would have as princes and princesses. Even though they were a royal family, they shared a lot of the same feelings and concerns that any parents would have, making sure their children were loved and well cared for.

The Great Exhibition

"It is not what we have in life, but who we have in our life that matters."
Queen Victoria

In the year 1851, something extraordinary happened in London—an event that would bring people from all over the world to see the wonders of invention and art. This event was called the Great Exhibition, and it was one of the most exciting moments of Queen Victoria's reign.

The idea for the Great Exhibition began with Prince Albert, Queen Victoria's beloved husband. Albert was a man of vision, and he believed that the world was full of amazing ideas and creations that should be shared and celebrated. He wanted to bring together the best of what people had made—from machines and tools to art and inventions—so that everyone could see how clever and creative people could be.

Queen Victoria loved Albert's idea. She knew that it would be a huge event, one that would make her country proud. Together, they began to plan the exhibition, and soon, all of Britain was buzzing with excitement. But they needed a special place to hold such a grand event—somewhere big enough to display all the wonders they wanted to show.

That's when they decided to build the Crystal Palace. The Crystal Palace was like nothing anyone had ever seen before. It was a giant building made almost entirely of glass, with a metal frame that sparkled in the sunlight. The palace was so large that it could fit thousands of people inside at once, and its glass walls made it look like a magical castle from a fairy tale. When people first saw it, they couldn't believe their eyes—it was truly a sight to behold.

Inside the Crystal Palace, there were treasures from all over the world. There were marvelous machines that could do all sorts of things, like spinning cotton or printing books. There were beautiful pieces of art, delicate jewelry, and colorful fabrics from distant lands. There were even strange and fascinating inventions, like a machine that could make ice and a model of a steam-powered carriage.

People came from far and wide to see the Great Exhibition. Some traveled by train, others by ship, all eager to catch a glimpse of the wonders inside the Crystal Palace. As they walked through the grand halls, they marveled at the displays, their eyes wide with wonder. It was like walking through a dream, where every corner revealed something new and amazing.

Queen Victoria and Prince Albert visited the exhibition many times. Victoria was so proud of what they had accomplished. She loved seeing the joy and excitement on people's faces as they explored the exhibits. She knew that this event was more than just a display of objects—it was a celebration of human achievement and the power of imagination.

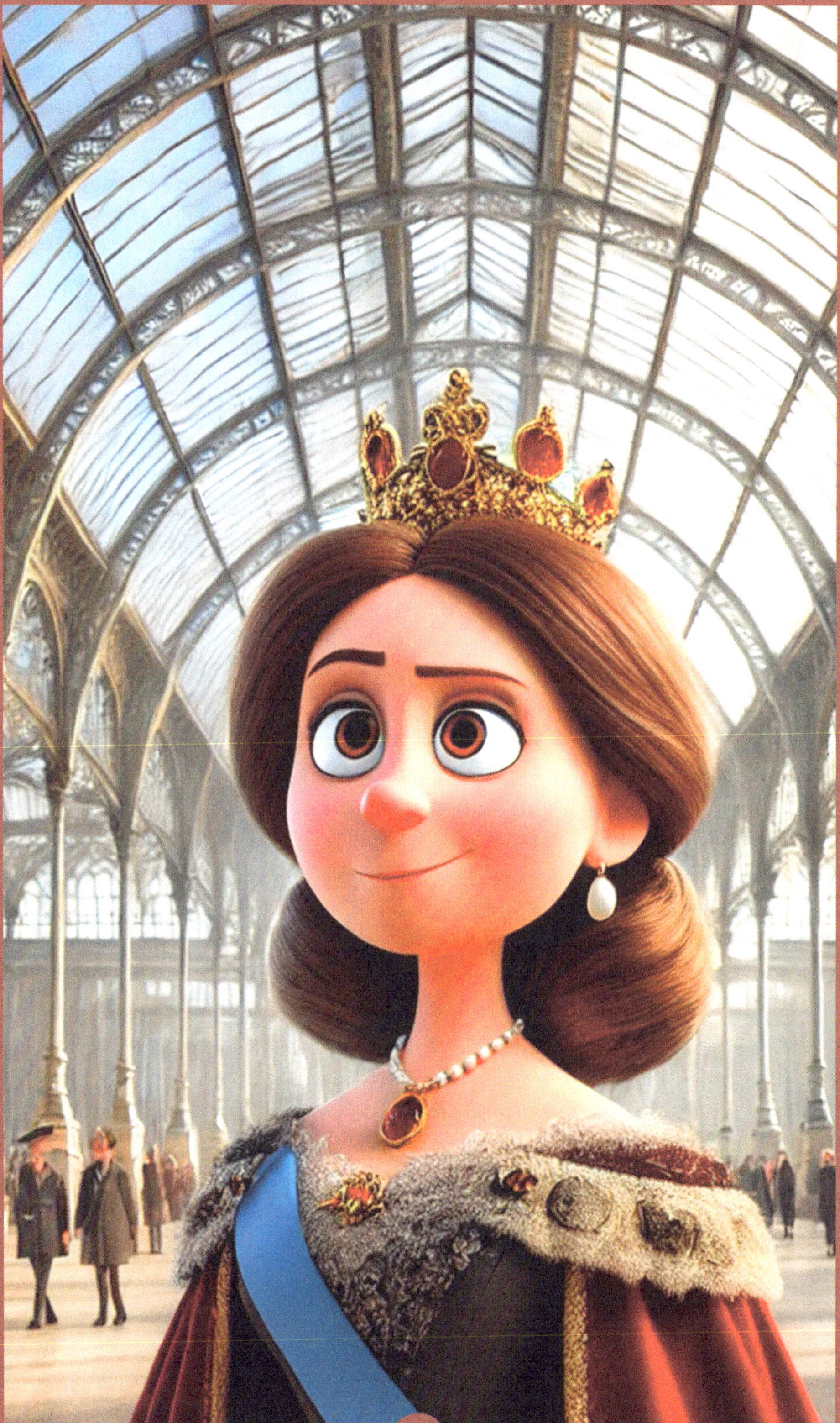

The Great Exhibition was a huge success. It showed the world that Britain was a place of innovation and creativity, where new ideas were born and shared. People left the Crystal Palace inspired, filled with new ideas and dreams of what they could create.

For Queen Victoria, the success of the Great Exhibition was one of the proudest moments of her reign. It brought the world together in a way that had never been done before, and it showed that when people work together, they can achieve great things. The Crystal Palace stood as a symbol of this spirit—shining brightly in the heart of London, a beacon of hope and progress.

The memories of the Great Exhibition stayed with Victoria for the rest of her life. She often thought back to those magical days, when the world came together to celebrate the best of what people could do. And every time she did, she felt a warm glow of pride, knowing that she and Albert had created something truly special—something that would be remembered for generations to come.

Fascinating Facts about Queen Victoria's Hobbies:

Drawing and Painting - Queen Victoria had a special hobby that she loved: drawing and painting. She enjoyed spending time with her pencils and paintbrushes, making beautiful pictures. Victoria often drew sketches and painted watercolors, which are paintings made with water-based colors. She loved making pictures of her children, her husband, Prince Albert, and even her pets. Sometimes, she would also draw the places she visited, like beautiful gardens, castles, and countryside scenes. Victoria was very good at drawing and painting, and she took great care with her artwork. She kept many of her drawings in special books called albums, where she could look at them whenever she wanted. These albums were like her own personal collections of memories, filled with the people and places she loved. Drawing and painting helped Queen Victoria relax and have fun, and it was a way for her to show how much she cared about the people and things that were important to her.

Writing in Her Journal – Queen Victoria had another special hobby: writing in her journal. A journal is like a diary where you can write down your thoughts, feelings, and what happens each day. Victoria started writing in her journal when she was just a young girl, and she kept writing in it almost every day for most of her life.

In her journal, Victoria would write about all sorts of things. She might describe what she did that day, who she met, and how she was feeling. Sometimes she wrote about important events, like meetings with other royals or big decisions she had to make as queen. Other times, she would write about her family, her children, and what she enjoyed doing.

Victoria's journals were very detailed, which means she wrote a lot about what was happening in her life. Because she kept writing for so many years, her journals are now a very important record. They help us understand what life was like when she was queen, what she thought about different events, and how she felt about the people around her.

By reading Victoria's journals, we can learn a lot about history and about her as a person. Writing in her journal was a way for Victoria to reflect on her day and express her feelings, and it became a lifelong habit that she enjoyed.

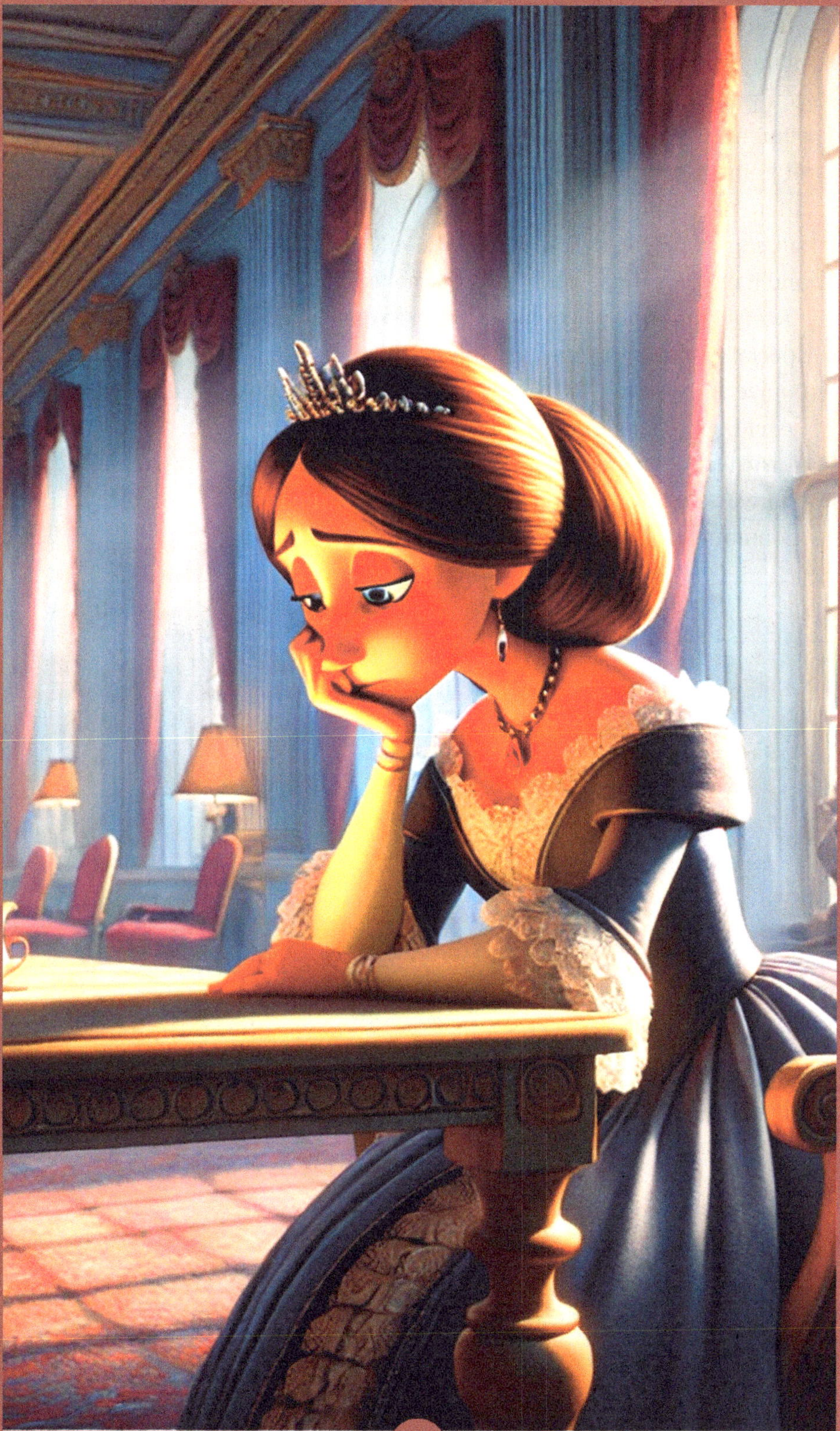

Music - Queen Victoria loved music very much. She enjoyed playing the piano, which is a musical instrument with black and white keys that you press to make music. Victoria also liked to sing, and music was something she shared with her husband, Prince Albert.

At home, music was a big part of Victoria and Albert's life. They would often play music together, with Victoria on the piano and Albert singing or playing another instrument. It was a way for them to relax and have fun, and it made their home feel lively and full of joy.

Victoria and Albert also loved going to concerts and operas, which are special performances where musicians play instruments or sing. They enjoyed listening to the beautiful sounds of the orchestra and watching the singers perform on stage.

Music was very important to Queen Victoria. It brought her happiness and was a way for her to connect with her husband and enjoy special moments together.

Reading - Queen Victoria loved to read. She was an avid reader, which means she really enjoyed spending time with books. Victoria liked reading about many different topics. She read history books to learn about the past, poetry to enjoy beautiful words and feelings, and novels, which are stories made up by authors.

Reading was something Victoria did often to relax. Even though she was very busy as a queen, she always made time to sit down with a good book. Reading helped her learn new things and escape into different worlds created by the stories she read.

Books were like a special friend to Victoria, always there to keep her company and help her explore new ideas. Whether it was learning about history or getting lost in a story, reading was one of Victoria's favorite ways to spend her time.

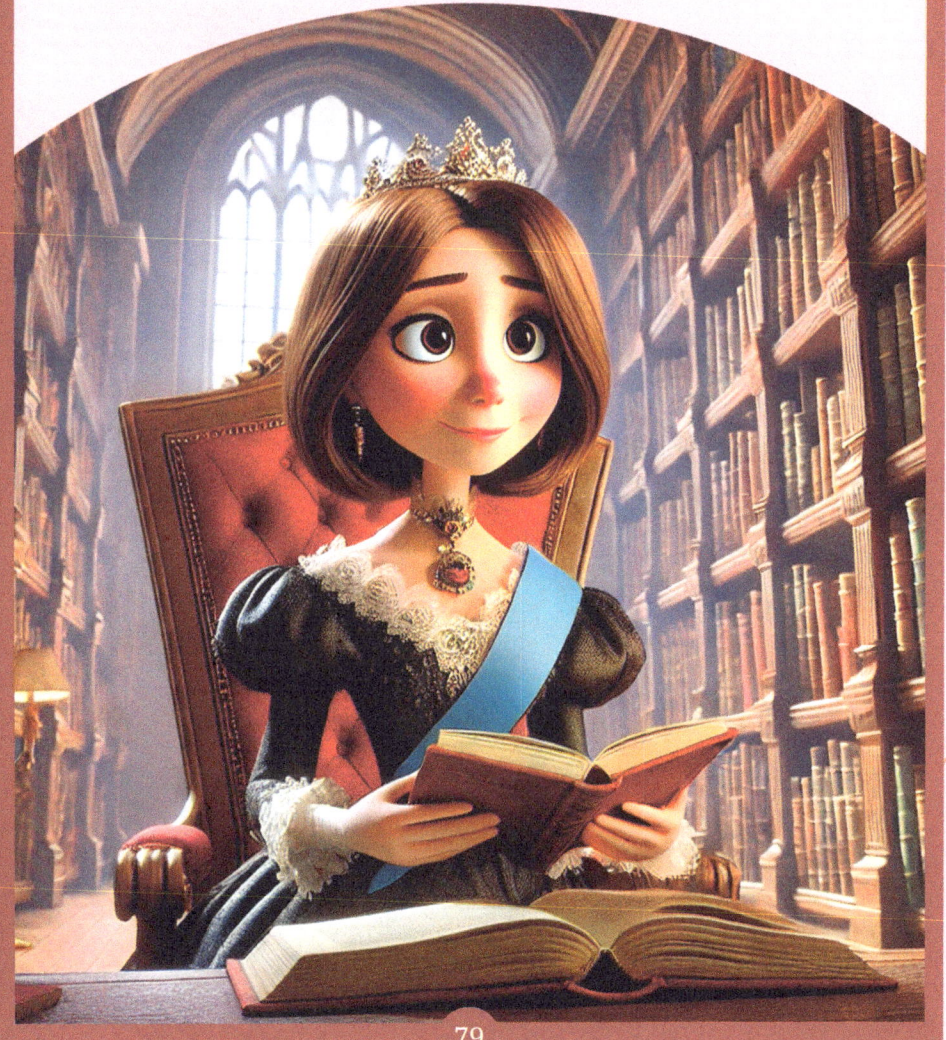

Horseback Riding - Queen Victoria loved horseback riding, especially when she was younger. Riding horses was one of her favorite activities because it allowed her to spend time outside and enjoy nature.

She would often go horseback riding in the parks around London, where she lived. Sometimes, she would ride at her country homes, where there was plenty of open space and beautiful scenery. Riding made Victoria feel free and happy, and it was a way for her to take a break from her royal duties.

When she was on a horse, she could explore the outdoors, feel the fresh air, and see the world from a different perspective. Horseback riding was not only fun for Victoria, but it also helped her stay active and healthy. It was a special hobby that brought her a lot of joy.

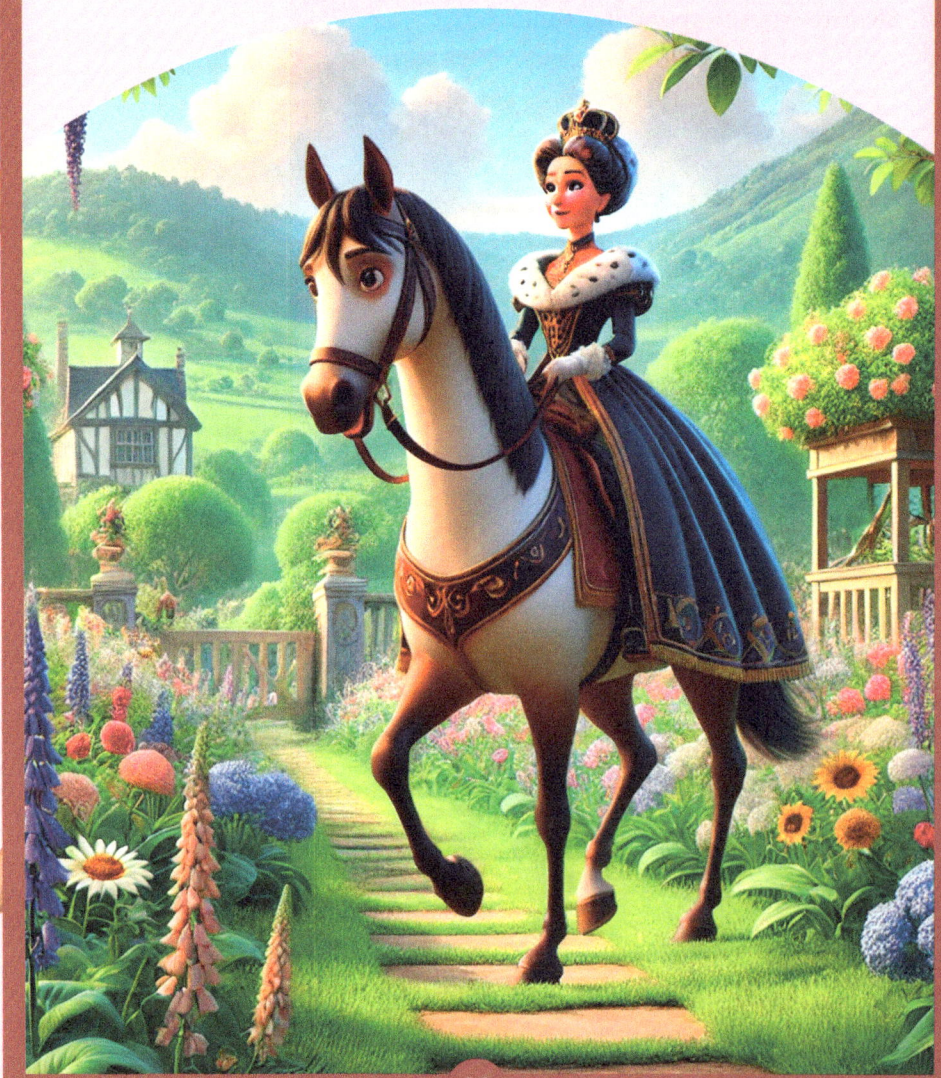

Collecting - Queen Victoria had a fun hobby of collecting things. One of her favorite collections was dolls. She started collecting dolls when she was a little girl, and even when she grew up, she kept adding more dolls to her collection. Her dolls were very special to her, and she loved looking at them and arranging them.

Victoria didn't just collect dolls; she also liked to collect souvenirs from the places she visited. A souvenir is a little item that helps you remember a special trip or place. Whenever Victoria traveled to a new place, she would bring back something to remind her of her visit.

She also received many gifts from people around the world, and she enjoyed adding these to her collection. Each item in her collection had a story behind it, making it even more special to her.

Collecting was a way for Queen Victoria to keep memories of her favorite things and places. Her collections were like little treasures that helped her remember the happy times in her life.

Queen Victoria's Love for the Scottish Highlands - Queen Victoria had a special place in her heart for Scotland, especially the Highlands. She loved the natural beauty and peacefulness of the region so much that she and her husband, Prince Albert, decided to buy Balmoral Castle in Aberdeenshire. Balmoral became a favorite retreat for the royal family, where they could escape the busy life of the royal court and enjoy the serenity of the Scottish countryside. Victoria's affection for Scotland grew even stronger due to her close relationship with John Brown, a Scottish servant who worked at Balmoral. John Brown became a trusted friend and companion to the queen, and their bond made her feel even more connected to the Highlands. This love for Scotland left a lasting legacy, and Balmoral Castle is still a cherished royal residence today.

Queen Victoria's Love for Dogs - Queen Victoria was a true dog lover, and she had many dogs throughout her life. One breed she was especially fond of was the Pomeranian. These small, fluffy dogs became very popular in England, thanks to the Queen's love for them. She had several Pomeranians, and they were often seen by her side. Victoria's affection for her dogs was well-known, and she treated them like members of the family. Her love for Pomeranians even influenced dog lovers across England, making the breed one of the most popular during her reign. Queen Victoria's fondness for dogs showed her caring and affectionate side, making her even more beloved by her people.

A Time of Sadness

"The old, if they are wise, will listen to the young."
Queen Victoria

Life was full of joy and adventure for Queen Victoria and Prince Albert. They had shared so many happy moments together, from raising their children to leading their country. But in the year 1861, something happened that changed everything—a great sadness that would stay with Victoria for the rest of her life.

One cold winter's day, Prince Albert became very ill. He had always been strong and full of energy, but now he was weak and tired. Doctors came to help, but there was little they could do. Victoria stayed by Albert's side, holding his hand and hoping with all her heart that he would get better. But day by day, he grew weaker.

Victoria was frightened. Albert was not just her husband; he was her best friend, her partner in everything. She couldn't imagine life without him. But despite all her hopes and prayers, Albert passed away on December 14, 1861. Victoria's heart was broken. She felt as though the light had gone out of her life.

After Albert's death, Victoria was filled with grief. She couldn't believe that he was gone, and the pain of losing him was almost too much to bear. To show how much she loved and missed him, Victoria decided to wear black every day for the rest of her life. Black became the color of her sorrow, a way to honor Albert and keep his memory close to her heart.

For a long time, Victoria couldn't find joy in anything. She withdrew from public life, spending most of her days in quiet solitude. She didn't want to attend parties or celebrations, and she rarely appeared in public. The palace, which had once been filled with laughter and music, was now silent and somber.

Victoria's children and advisors worried about her. They knew how much she missed Albert, but they also knew that the country needed its queen. They gently encouraged her to return to her duties, to show her people that she was still strong, even in her sadness.

Slowly, Victoria began to take on her royal responsibilities again. It wasn't easy—every day was a struggle without Albert by her side. But she knew that he would have wanted her to continue, to be the queen that her people needed. She held on to the love they had shared, using it as her strength to carry on.

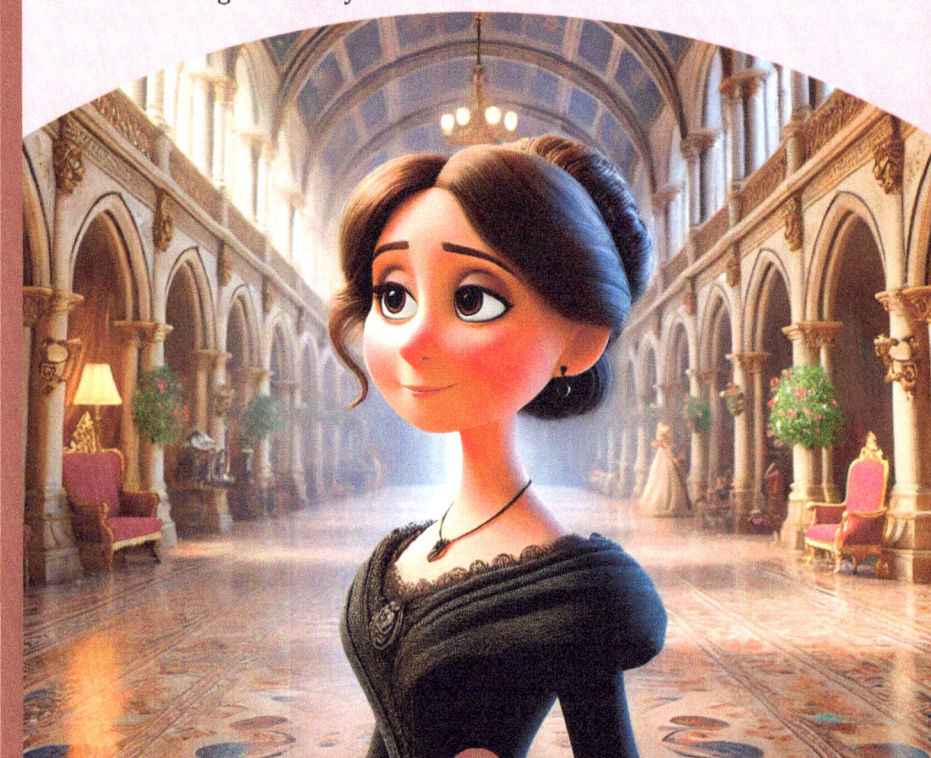

87

Though Victoria never stopped mourning Albert, she found comfort in the memories they had made together. She kept his room in the palace just as it had been when he was alive, and she often visited places they had loved, like their home in Balmoral, Scotland. In these quiet moments, she felt close to him again, as if he were still with her in spirit. Victoria's love for Albert never faded. Even as she grew older, she continued to honor him in every way she could. She made sure that people remembered him, not just as a prince, but as a kind and wise man who had done so much for his country. The time of sadness after Albert's death was one of the hardest in Victoria's life. But through her grief, she found a way to keep going. She learned that even though someone you love may no longer be with you, the love you shared never truly goes away. It stays in your heart, giving you the strength to face each new day. And so, while Victoria's heart remained heavy with sorrow, she also found peace in knowing that Albert's memory would live on forever—in her heart, in their children, and in the country they had both loved so dearly.

Fascinating Facts about Queen Victoria's Habits:

Early Riser - Queen Victoria had a habit of waking up early in the morning. She was what we call an "early riser," which means she liked to get out of bed as soon as the sun came up. Victoria believed that starting her day early gave her more time to do all the important things she needed to do as a queen.

By waking up early, she could plan her day, take care of her royal duties, and still have time for her hobbies. It helped her stay organized and feel in control of her busy life. Victoria thought that getting up early was one of the reasons she could be such a good queen, because it allowed her to get a lot done each day.

Tea Time - Queen Victoria loved drinking tea, just like many people in Britain. She had a special habit of enjoying "afternoon tea." This was a time in the afternoon when she would have a light meal with a cup of tea and some tasty snacks.

Afternoon tea might include little sandwiches, cakes, and biscuits, which are like cookies. It was a relaxing and enjoyable part of her day, where she could take a break and enjoy some delicious treats.

Because Queen Victoria loved afternoon tea so much, it became a popular tradition in Britain.

Many people started having afternoon tea just like she did, and it's a tradition that people still enjoy today. When you have tea and snacks in the afternoon, you're sharing in a tradition that Queen Victoria helped make famous!

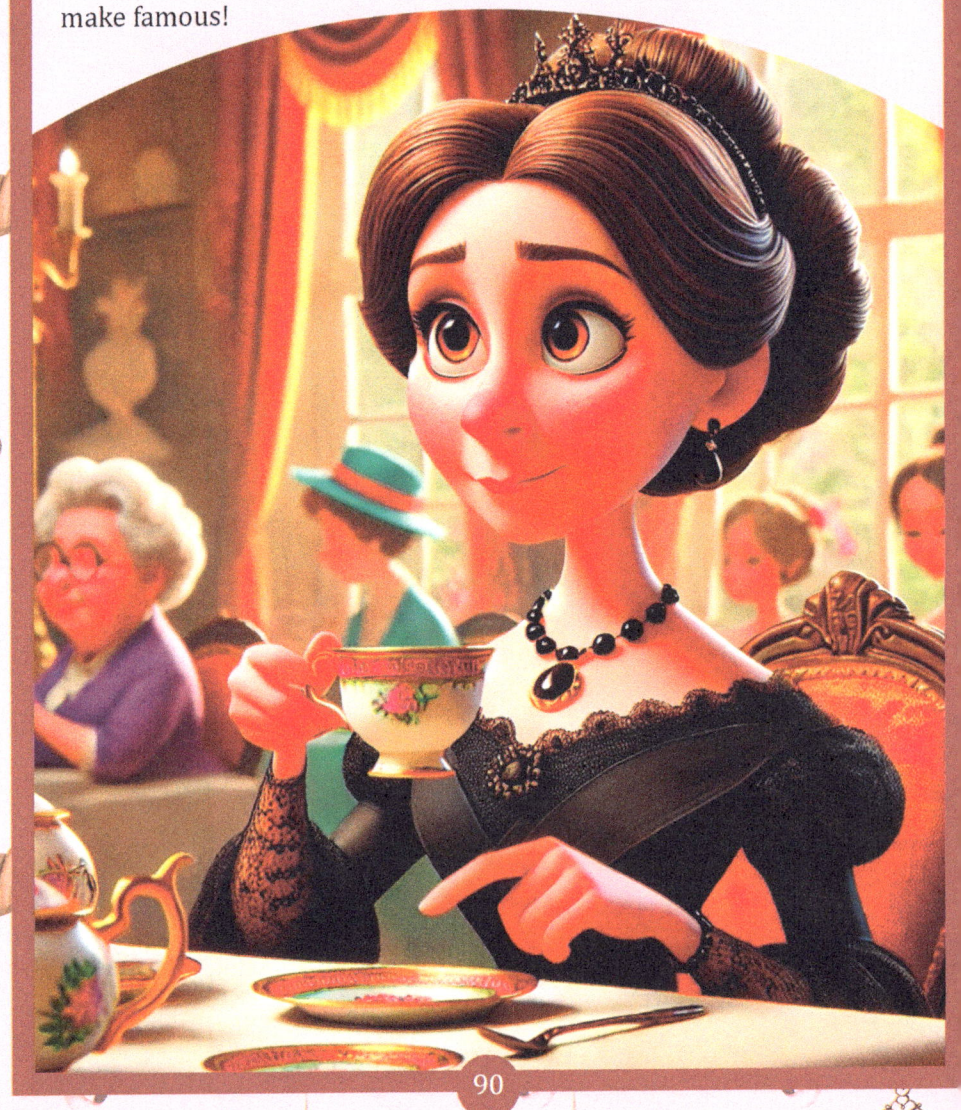

Long Walks - Queen Victoria loved taking long walks, especially when she was staying at her country homes, which were large houses in the countryside. She believed that walking was good for her health because it kept her body strong and fit.

Victoria liked to spend time outside in nature, where she could breathe in the fresh air and enjoy the beautiful scenery around her. During her walks, she had time to think about important things, make decisions, or just relax and clear her mind. Walking was one of her favorite ways to feel calm and happy.

These long walks helped Queen Victoria stay healthy and gave her a peaceful break from her busy life as a queen.

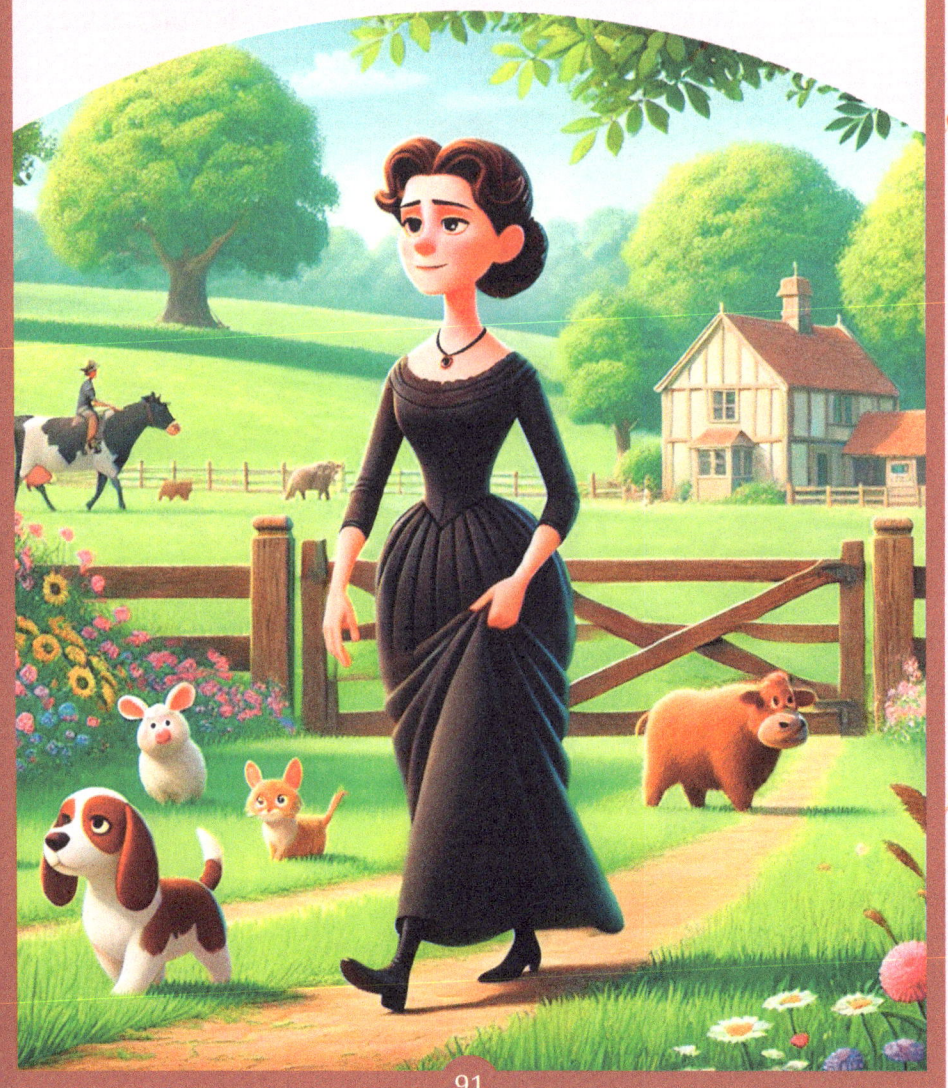

Dinner Etiquette - Queen Victoria cared a lot about dinner etiquette, which means she had strict rules for how things should be done during meals. She believed that meals should be orderly and polite, and she wanted everyone at her dinner table to follow these rules.

For example, Queen Victoria had specific places where each person should sit at the table. She also expected everyone to behave properly, which meant talking politely, sitting up straight, and not interrupting others. There were even rules about how to use the utensils, like forks and knives, and the proper way to eat each type of food.

Victoria's rules helped make dinners feel special and respectful. She believed that following good manners at the table was important, and she wanted everyone around her to do the same. These dinner rules showed how much she valued order and politeness, and they helped make her meals elegant and dignified occasions.

Writing Letters - Queen Victoria had a special habit of writing letters every day. In those days, there were no phones or emails, so writing letters was the best way to stay in touch with people.

Victoria would write letters to her family, friends, and other important people, like leaders from different countries. It was her way of keeping connected with the people she cared about, even if they were far away. By writing letters, Victoria could share her thoughts, ask questions, and tell others about what was happening in her life. She wrote so many letters that it became a daily routine for her, just like brushing your teeth or getting dressed.

Writing letters helped Queen Victoria communicate and build strong relationships with others, and it was a big part of her life.

Personal Appearance - Queen Victoria paid a lot of attention to how she looked. She always made sure to dress in a way that was right for her role as queen. This meant wearing clothes that were elegant and showed her importance as a leader.

After her husband, Prince Albert, died, Victoria was very sad and wanted to show her sorrow. She decided to wear black clothes as a sign of mourning, which means feeling and showing grief for someone who has passed away. Wearing black was her way of honoring Prince Albert and remembering him.

The Widow of Windsor

"Courage does not mean not being frightened, but being able to do what is right, even when you are afraid."
Queen Victoria

After the sad passing of Prince Albert, Queen Victoria was often called the "Widow of Windsor." Windsor was the grand castle where she spent much of her time, and "widow" means someone who has lost their husband. Though her heart was heavy with grief, Victoria knew she still had a great responsibility as Queen. The people of Britain needed her, and slowly, she began to return to her duties.

Victoria continued to wear black every day as a sign of her mourning for Albert. But even as she grieved, she found the strength to lead her country. Her love for Albert gave her the courage to keep going, and she dedicated herself to the work of being a queen. She met with important leaders, made decisions for her people, and showed that she was still strong, even in her sadness. During these years, Victoria formed a special friendship with one of her servants, a man named John Brown. John was a loyal and kind-hearted Scottish servant who worked at Balmoral, the castle in Scotland where Victoria and Albert had spent many happy times together. After Albert's death, John became a close companion to the Queen. He was always there to support her, whether she needed someone to talk to or simply a steady hand to guide her. John Brown was different from the other servants. He was straightforward and didn't treat Victoria like a distant queen, but rather as a person who needed care and friendship. He made her laugh when she was feeling sad and helped her find joy in little things, like taking long walks in the Scottish hills or riding horses through the countryside. Victoria valued John's companionship deeply, and their friendship brought her comfort during her loneliest days.

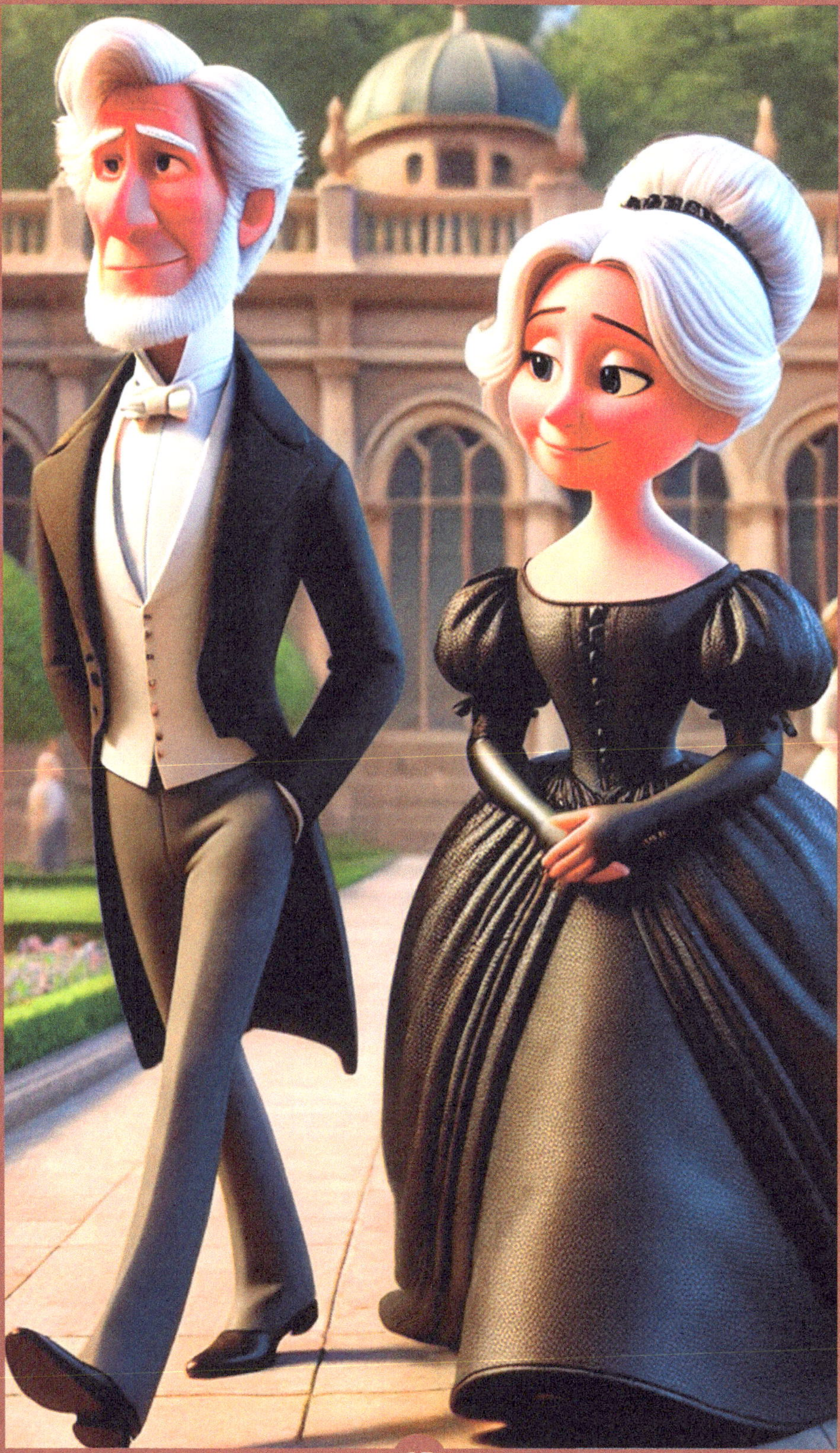

Despite her private sorrows, Victoria remained a powerful figure in British life. People admired her strength and dedication. They saw how she continued to rule with wisdom and care, even while mourning the loss of her beloved Albert. Victoria became known as the "Widow of Windsor" because of the way she balanced her personal grief with her public duties. She showed everyone that even in the darkest times, it was possible to find the strength to carry on. Victoria's role as queen continued to grow. She became an important symbol for her people, not just in Britain but around the world. Other countries respected her, and her reign became a time of great progress for Britain. Victoria was proud of what her country had achieved, and she knew that Albert would have been proud too. As the years passed, Victoria's family grew, with her children marrying and having children of their own. Her many grandchildren were spread across Europe, and they often visited her at Windsor Castle. These visits brought her joy and reminded her of the happy times she had spent with Albert and their own children. Though her life was not as it once had been, Victoria found peace in her family and in the work she did for her country.

Victoria's later years were marked by a quiet strength. She was no longer the young queen who had danced and laughed at grand balls, but a wise and experienced ruler who had faced many challenges. She had lived through both joy and sorrow, and she had come out stronger on the other side.

Even as she grew older, Victoria continued to be loved by her people. They admired her for her bravery, her dedication, and the way she had never given up, even when life was hard. To them, she was not just a queen, but a true leader who had shown them the importance of courage and resilience. And so, Queen Victoria, the Widow of Windsor, lived on in the hearts of her people. She was a queen who had loved deeply, mourned deeply, and led her country with unwavering strength. Her legacy would be remembered for generations, a testament to the power of love, duty, and the enduring spirit of a queen who never gave up.

Fascinating Facts about the Appearance of Queen Victoria:

Petite Stature - Queen Victoria was known for being quite small in size. She was only 4 feet 11 inches tall, which is about 1.50 meters. This means she wasn't very tall, even as an adult.

But even though she was short, Queen Victoria had a strong and powerful presence. People respected her a lot, and she knew how to make herself heard and seen. As she got older, she became even more confident and strong in her role as queen.

So, even though she was small in stature, she was big in the way she led her country and the way people admired her.

Youthful Features - When Queen Victoria was young, she was known for having a fresh, rosy complexion, which means her skin looked healthy and had a slight pink color. She also had blue eyes and brown hair. These features made her look very youthful and full of life.

Because she was small in size and had such a youthful appearance, Victoria looked innocent and approachable. This means people found her friendly and easy to talk to. This was different from the way most people imagined a king or queen, who were often thought of as serious and distant.

Victoria's youthful look made her seem more like an ordinary person, which helped people feel closer to her, even though she was a queen.

Weight Gain - As Queen Victoria got older, her body became heavier, especially after she had many children and went through the difficult time of losing her husband, Prince Albert. By the time she reached middle age, people could see that she had gained weight.

This change happened for a few reasons. After Prince Albert died, Victoria felt very sad and started to eat more for comfort, which is something people sometimes do when they are feeling upset. She also became less active and spent more time sitting or staying indoors, which is called having a sedentary lifestyle.

Because of these changes, Victoria's figure became more robust, or fuller, and this was something people often noticed and talked about when they described her.

Hair and Veils - In her later years, Queen Victoria's hair turned white, which is what happens as people get older. She often wore her white hair pulled back neatly and covered with a special white widow's cap or a bonnet. A widow's cap is a kind of hat that covers the hair, and a bonnet is a soft, rounded hat that ties under the chin.

Victoria also liked to wear a small lace veil over her cap or bonnet. A lace veil is a delicate, see-through cloth that she draped over her head. Even when she was attending important events or formal occasions, she kept this look. This style of wearing her hair and the lace veil became a signature part of her appearance as she grew older. It was a way for her to maintain a dignified and recognizable look, while also showing that she was still in mourning for her husband, Prince Albert.

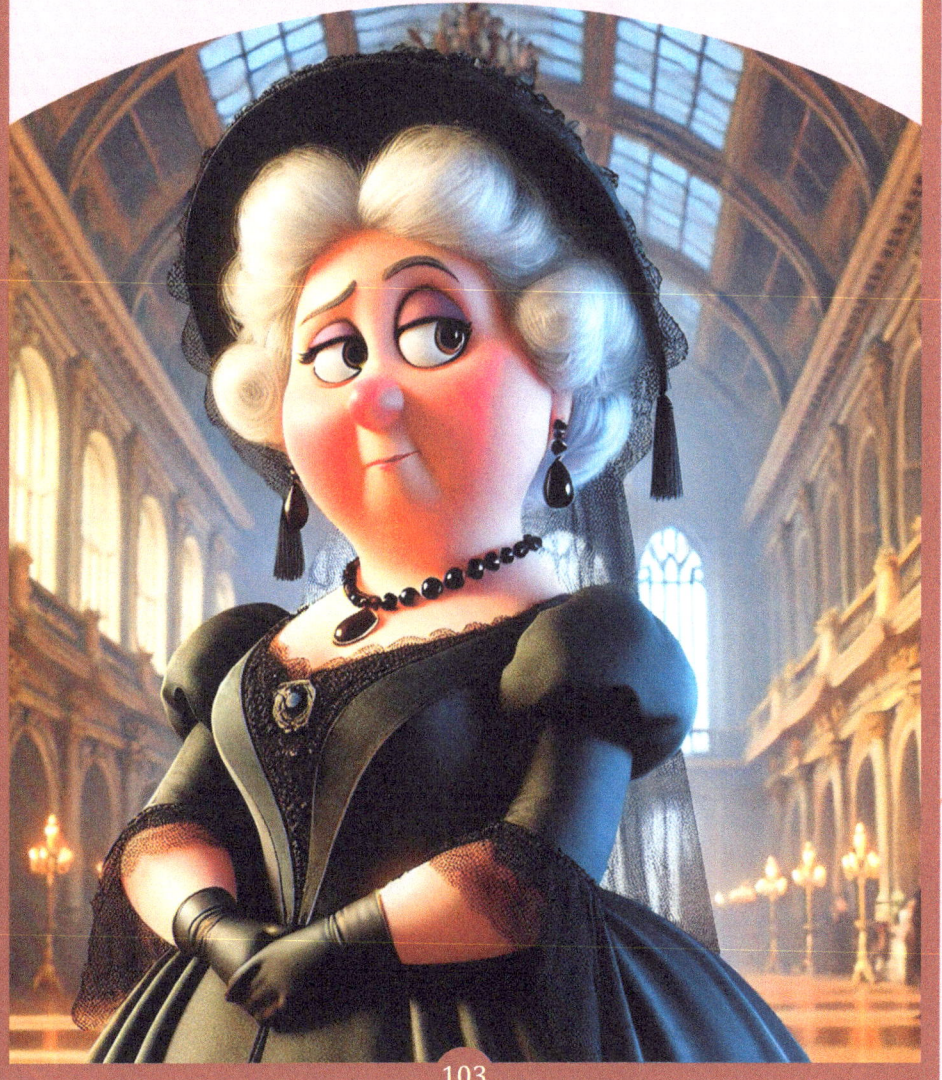

Minimal Makeup - Queen Victoria liked to keep her look very natural. She wore very little makeup, which was a part of the Victorian ideals of modesty and purity. This means she believed in showing her true self without using a lot of cosmetics or artificial beauty products.

While some women of her time used a lot of makeup to enhance their appearance, Victoria chose a simpler style. She felt that wearing minimal makeup was a way to show her natural beauty and remain modest. Her preference for a natural look made her stand out from others who might have used more elaborate cosmetics.

By keeping her makeup minimal, Queen Victoria stayed true to her values and set an example of simplicity and elegance.

Empress of India

"Where there is love, there is hope."
Queen Victoria

As the years passed, Queen Victoria's role as a leader continued to grow. She had already been the queen of Britain for many years, but in 1876, something very special happened—she was given a new title that made her feel proud and excited. Victoria was named the Empress of India, a title that showed just how large and powerful the British Empire had become.

India was a beautiful and fascinating country, full of rich history, colorful traditions, and diverse cultures. Although Victoria had never visited India herself, she was deeply curious about it. She wanted to learn everything she could about this faraway land that was now part of her empire.

Victoria's new title was more than just words—it was a sign of how much the British Empire had expanded during her reign. The empire stretched across the globe, from the green hills of England to the vast plains of India, and many other places in between. As Empress of India, Victoria felt a great responsibility to learn about the people and cultures of her empire, and to show them that she cared.

One of the ways Victoria connected with India was through the people who came from there to serve in her household. She developed close friendships with her Indian servants, who taught her about their homeland. They told her stories about the festivals, food, and customs of India, and Victoria listened with great interest.

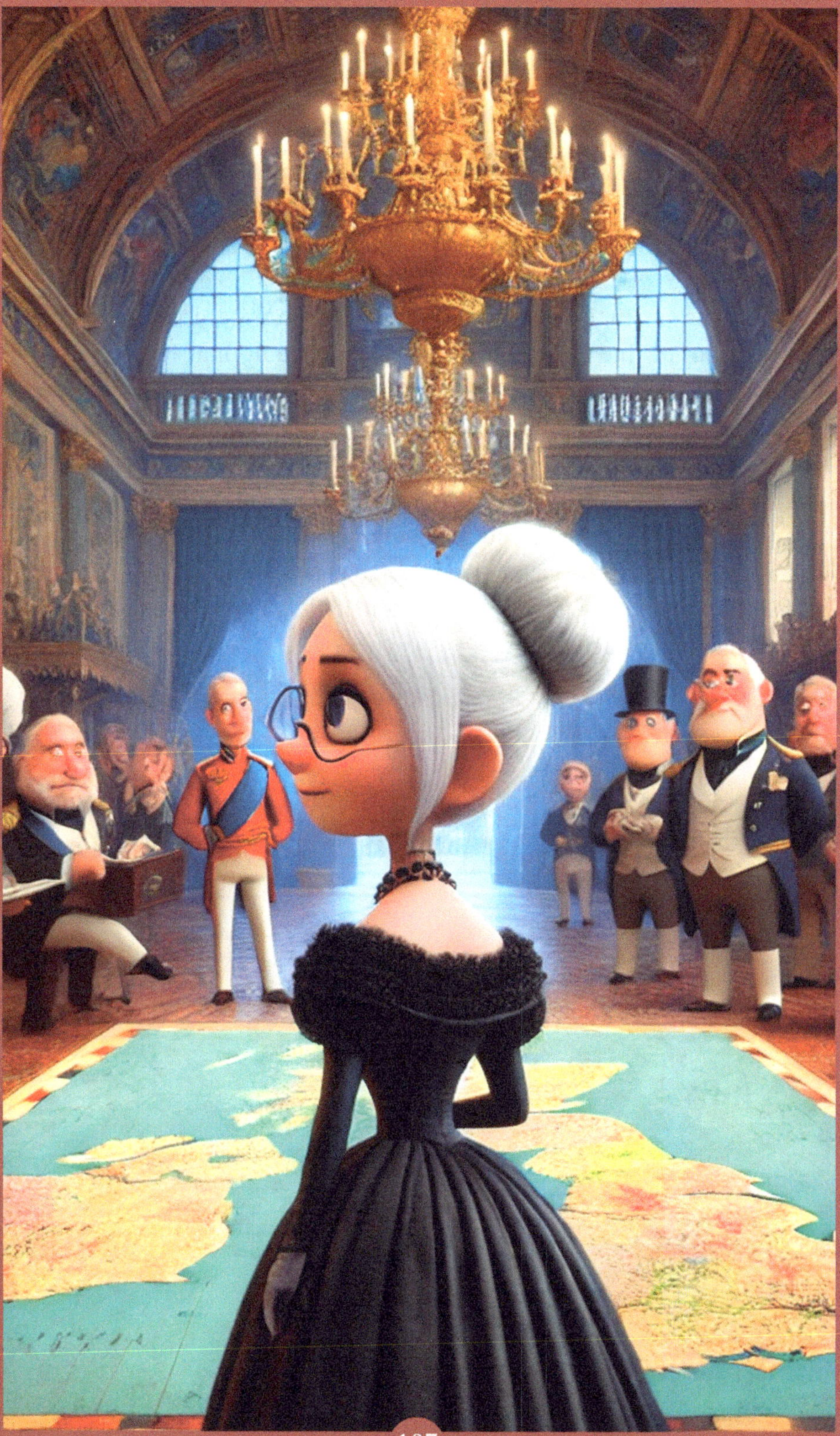

Victoria's fascination with India grew stronger every day. She was especially interested in learning the Hindi language, so she could better understand the stories and poems that were shared with her. Even though Hindi was very different from English, Victoria worked hard to learn it, practicing the words and phrases with her Indian friends. She enjoyed learning new things, and it made her feel closer to the people of India. The Queen also loved celebrating Indian festivals, which were full of music, dance, and bright colors. She would sometimes join in the celebrations at her palace, decorating her rooms with beautiful Indian fabrics and enjoying traditional Indian foods. These moments made her feel connected to the land she had never seen, but had grown to love through the stories and traditions shared with her. As Empress of India, Victoria wanted to show her respect and admiration for the country and its people. She supported many projects that helped India, such as building schools and hospitals, and she encouraged the exchange of knowledge between Britain and India. She believed that even though the countries were far apart, they could learn a lot from each other.

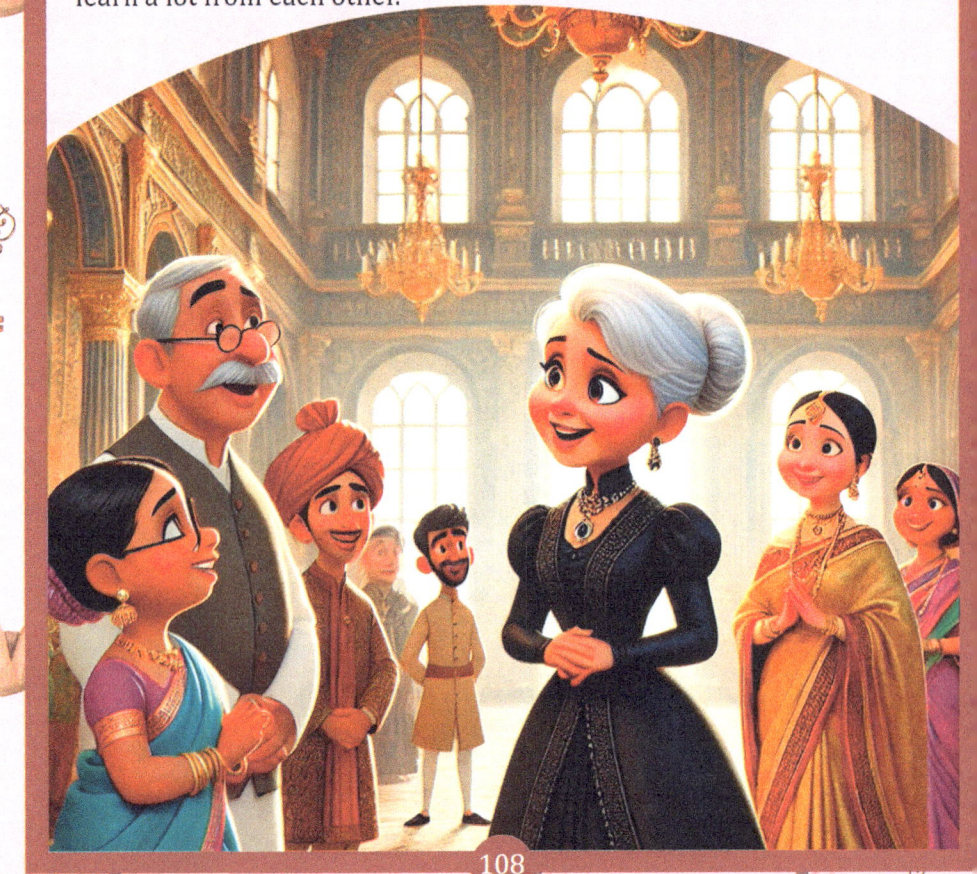

Victoria's interest in India was not just about power—it was about understanding and friendship. She knew that being an empress meant more than just ruling over a land; it meant caring for its people and appreciating their culture. Her efforts to learn about India and her friendships with her Indian servants showed that she wanted to be a thoughtful and kind leader, even from across the ocean.

Throughout her reign, Victoria's title as Empress of India remained one of her most cherished honors. It reminded her of the vastness of the empire she ruled, and of the many different people who lived within it. She often thought of India, imagining the bustling markets, the serene temples, and the vibrant festivals that she had come to admire.

Queen Victoria's love for India and her efforts to connect with its people were a significant part of her legacy. She showed the world that being a leader was not just about holding power, but about understanding and respecting the cultures and people within your care.

And so, as Empress of India, Victoria added another chapter to her remarkable life. She had ruled over a growing empire with wisdom and grace, always seeking to learn and grow, and to bring people closer together, no matter how far apart they were. Her reign was a shining example of how curiosity, kindness, and respect can build bridges between different cultures, making the world a more connected and understanding place.

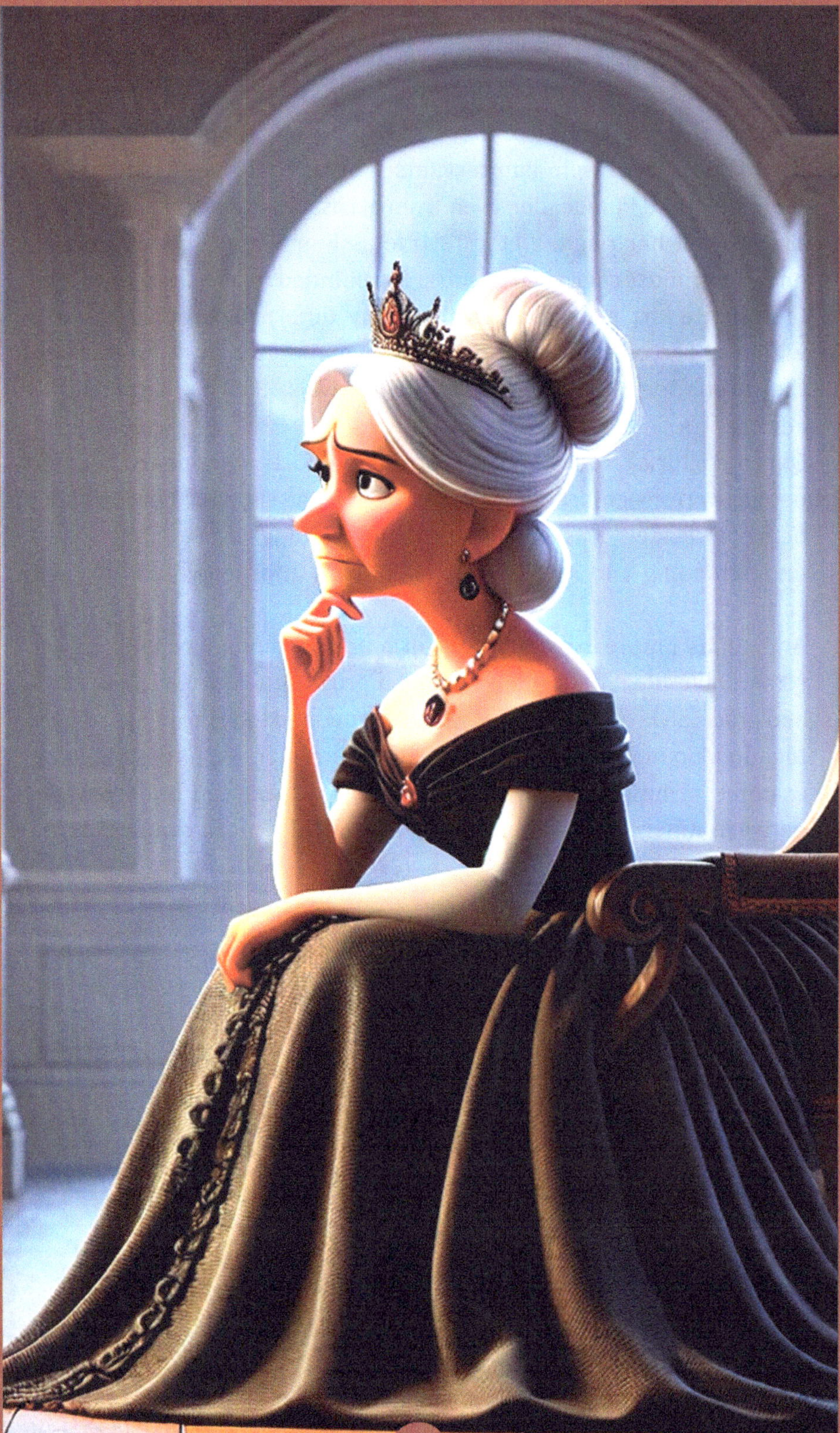

Fascinating Facts about Queen Victoria's Favorite Foods:

Simple Comfort Foods - Queen Victoria really liked simple and comforting foods. These are the kinds of meals that make you feel cozy and happy. One of her favorite dishes was roast beef. Roast beef is a popular British meal where beef is cooked slowly until it's tender and juicy. It's a big, hearty dish that fills you up and makes you feel satisfied.

Victoria also enjoyed other traditional meals that were both hearty and satisfying. These kinds of foods are usually warm and filling, which makes them perfect for a comforting meal. Even though she was a queen, she loved these down-to-earth, tasty dishes that made her feel good.

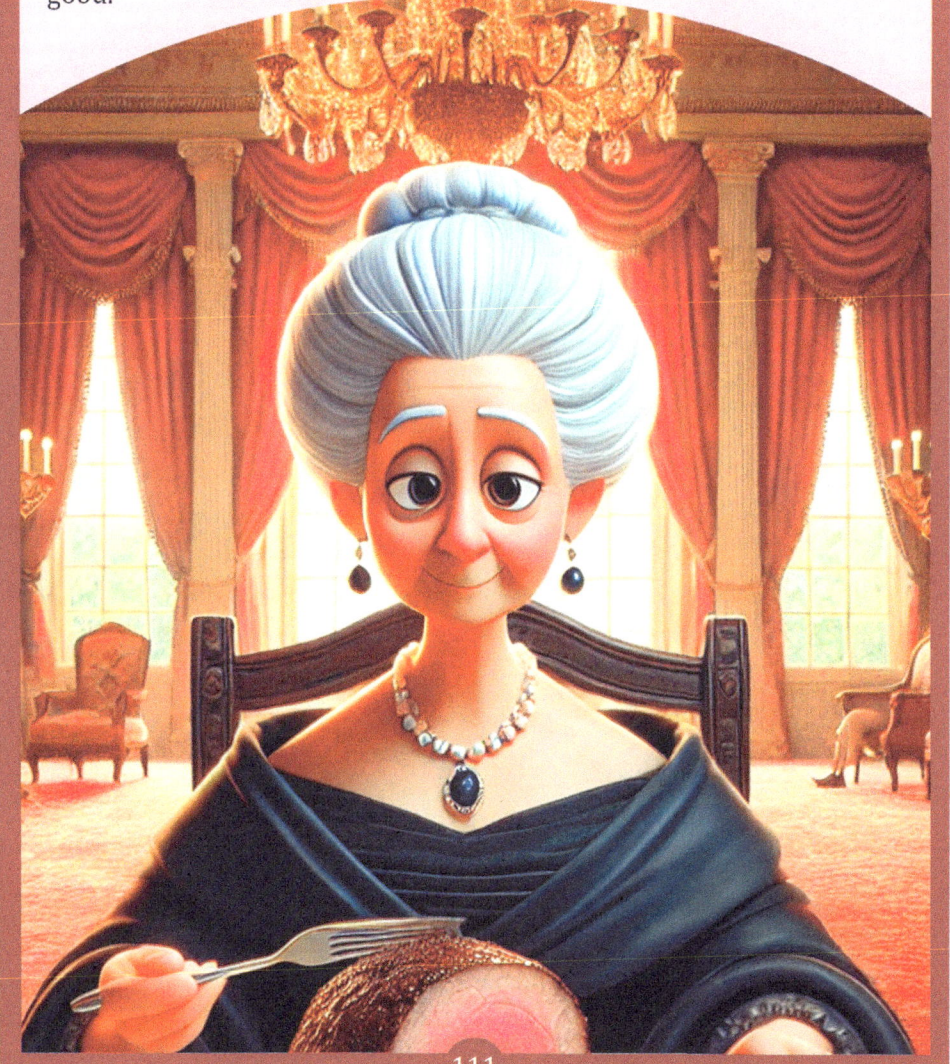

Love for Potatoes - Queen Victoria really loved potatoes! Potatoes are a type of vegetable that can be cooked in lots of different ways. Victoria enjoyed eating them in many styles. For example, she liked mashed potatoes, which are soft and creamy, and roasted potatoes, which are crispy and golden.

Potatoes were a big part of her meals, and she ate them often. They are a simple and tasty food that can be served with many different dishes. Even as a queen, Victoria enjoyed the comfort and variety of potatoes, making them one of her favorite foods.

Afternoon Tea Treats - Queen Victoria loved her afternoon tea, which is a special time in the afternoon to relax and enjoy some tasty treats with tea. During her tea time, she liked to have a variety of delicious snacks.

One of her favorites was scones, which are soft, biscuit-like pastries. Scones taste even better when you spread them with clotted cream, a thick, rich cream, and sweet jam. Victoria also enjoyed eating cakes, which are sweet and come in many different flavors, and finger sandwiches, which are small sandwiches with the crusts cut off.

Afternoon tea was a time for Victoria to enjoy these yummy treats, making it a special and enjoyable part of her day.

Chocolate Delight - Queen Victoria really loved chocolate! She especially enjoyed chocolate cakes, which are sweet, rich, and full of chocolatey goodness. Chocolate was one of her favorite treats, and she would often have it as a special indulgence.

Since chocolate was such a favorite of hers, she enjoyed it on special occasions when she wanted something extra delicious. Whether it was in the form of a cake or just a simple treat, chocolate always made Victoria happy and was one of her favorite sweets to enjoy.

Fruit and Pastries - Queen Victoria loved eating fresh fruits and pastries. Some of her favorite fruits were apples and berries. Apples are crunchy and sweet, while berries are small, juicy, and full of flavor. These fruits were a refreshing part of her meals.

Victoria also enjoyed pastries, which are sweet baked goods. She liked tarts, which are pastries filled with fruit or creamy fillings, and pies, which can be filled with fruits like apples or other tasty ingredients. These delicious treats were often served at her meals, and she enjoyed them very much. Fruit and pastries added a sweet and satisfying touch to Queen Victoria's meals, making them some of her favorite foods.

Rich Sauces - Queen Victoria liked to add rich, flavorful sauces to her meals. One of her favorites was gravy, which is a sauce made from the juices left in the pan after cooking meat. Gravy is usually thickened and sometimes seasoned with herbs and spices, making it deliciously rich. Victoria enjoyed pouring gravy over her meals, especially with dishes like roast beef or mashed potatoes. The gravy added extra flavor and made the food taste even better. Having rich sauces like gravy was one of the ways Victoria liked to enjoy her meals, making them more flavorful and satisfying.

Seafood - Queen Victoria enjoyed eating seafood, which includes dishes made from fish and shellfish like shrimp and oysters. She liked the fresh taste of seafood, and it was often a part of her meals, especially when she was staying at her homes near the sea.

Seafood was a special treat for her because it was fresh and flavorful. Whether it was a simple fish dish or something more elaborate, Victoria enjoyed the variety that seafood brought to her dining experience. Eating seafood by the seaside made her meals even more enjoyable.

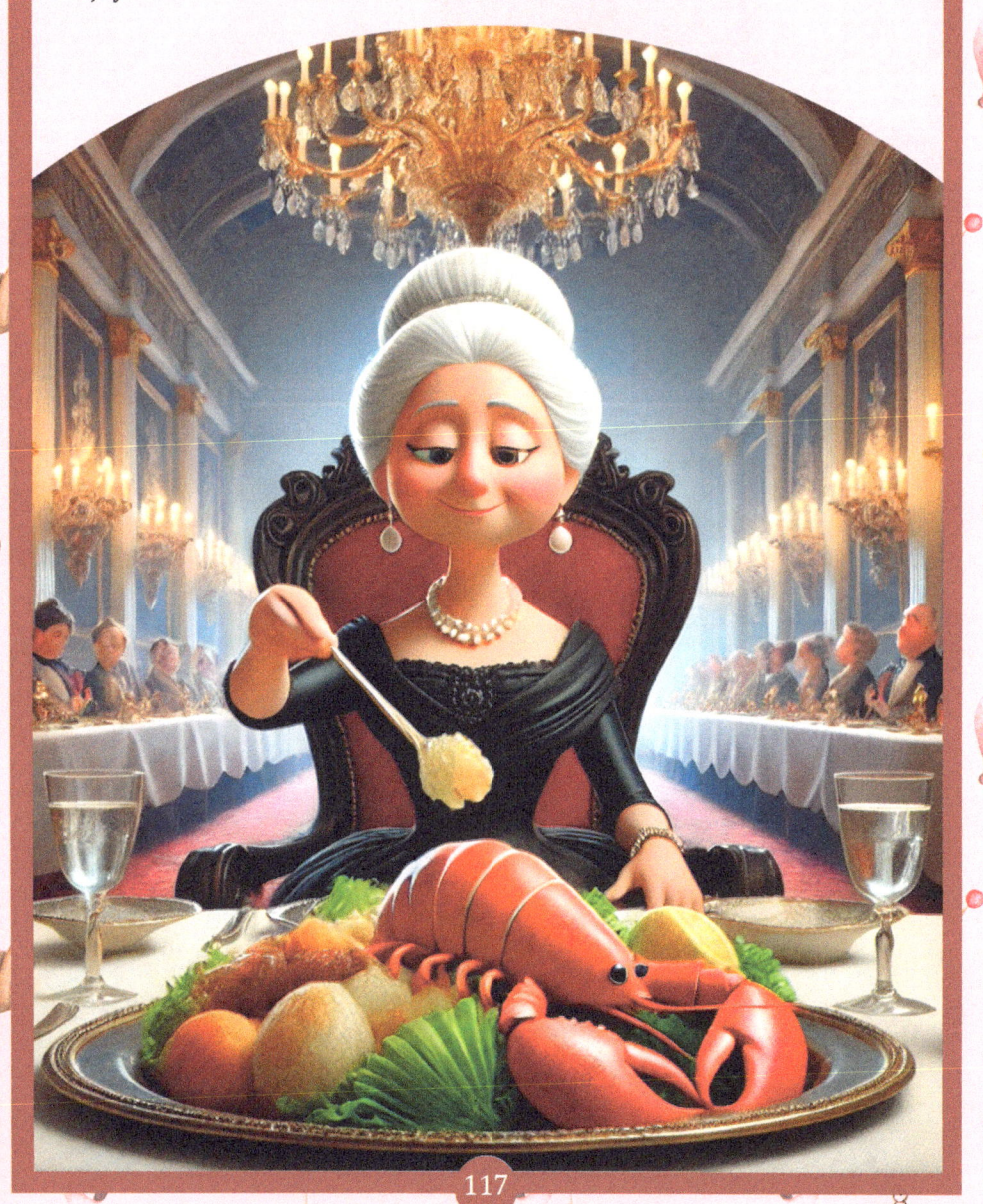

The Golden Jubilee

"Work is the true source of happiness."
Queen Victoria

In the summer of 1887, something truly magical happened in Britain. The whole country was buzzing with excitement, and there was a sense of joy in the air that couldn't be missed. It was a very special year—Queen Victoria was celebrating her Golden Jubilee, marking 50 years on the throne!

Fifty years as queen was a remarkable achievement, and everyone wanted to honor Victoria for her long and devoted reign. People from all over the world came to Britain to join in the celebrations. It wasn't just the British who admired her—Victoria was loved by people in many countries, and they all wanted to show their respect and gratitude.

The streets of London were decorated with flags, banners, and flowers. Everywhere you looked, there were signs of celebration. Crowds gathered, eager to catch a glimpse of their beloved queen as she made her way through the city in a grand parade. Victoria, dressed in elegant robes and wearing her sparkling crown, rode in a beautiful carriage.

The cheers of the people filled the air as they waved and shouted her name, celebrating the queen who had guided them for half a century. As Victoria passed by, she smiled and waved to the crowds. Her heart was full of pride and happiness. She had faced many challenges and sorrows over the years, but she had always remained strong for her people. Now, seeing how much they loved and appreciated her, she felt that all her efforts had been worth it.

The celebrations continued with grand parties and feasts held in Victoria's honor. Leaders and dignitaries from around the world came to pay their respects. They brought with them magnificent gifts, each one a symbol of the friendship and admiration they felt for the queen. There were jewels, paintings, and even special coins made just for the occasion. Each gift was a reminder of how much Victoria was loved, not just in Britain, but across the globe.

One of the most memorable events of the Golden Jubilee was a grand banquet held at Buckingham Palace. The palace was lit up with thousands of lights, and the grand halls were filled with music and laughter. Victoria sat at the head of the table, surrounded by her family, friends, and guests from far and wide. As she looked around the room, she felt a deep sense of accomplishment. She had seen her country grow and change in many ways, and she was proud of all that had been achieved during her reign.

But what touched Victoria the most was the way ordinary people celebrated her Jubilee. Across the country, people held their own parties and gatherings. They sang songs, danced, and shared stories about their queen. Some even lit bonfires in her honor, their flames reaching up to the sky like beacons of love and respect. Victoria knew that it was the love of her people that had given her the strength to lead for so many years.

Throughout the Jubilee celebrations, Victoria was reminded of all the important moments of her reign—the day she became queen, her marriage to Albert, the birth of her children, the triumphs, and the challenges. It had been a long journey, full of ups and downs, but standing there, surrounded by the love of her people, she knew it had been a journey worth taking.

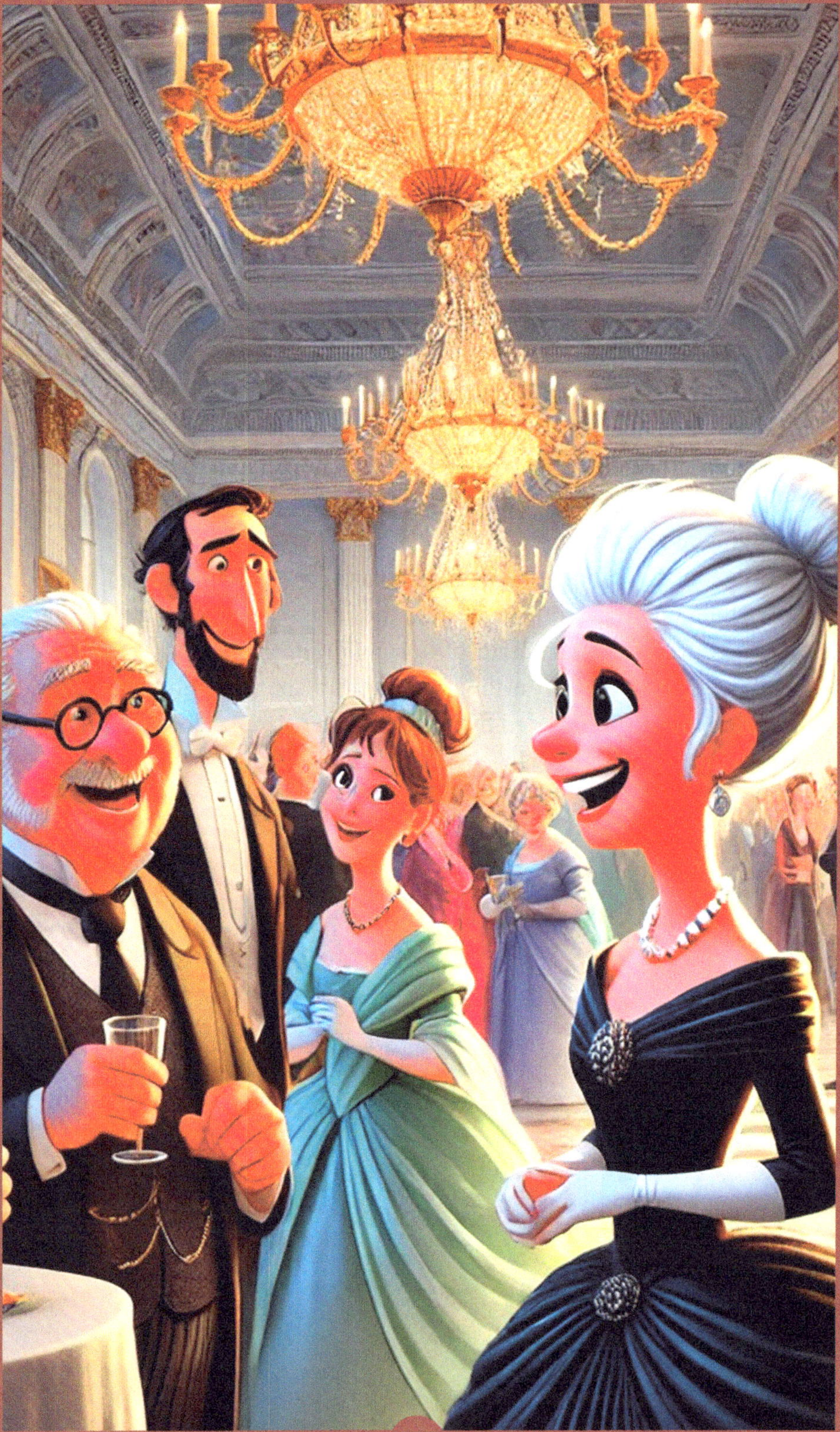

As the Golden Jubilee came to an end, Victoria reflected on the years that had passed. She thought about how much the world had changed since she first became queen, and how much she had learned along the way. But one thing had remained constant—the deep bond she shared with her people. It was a bond built on trust, respect, and love, and it was stronger than ever.

Queen Victoria's Golden Jubilee was more than just a celebration of her reign—it was a celebration of the remarkable woman she had become. She was no longer just a queen; she was a symbol of strength, resilience, and kindness. The people loved her not just for her crown, but for her heart.

And as the last fireworks lit up the night sky, Victoria knew that she would carry the memories of this special time with her forever. The Golden Jubilee was a shining moment in her life, a golden thread in the tapestry of her reign, woven with the love and loyalty of her people.

Fascinating Facts about Queen Victoria:

Surviving Eight Assassination Attempts - Even though Queen Victoria's reign is often remembered as a time when the British Royal Family regained popularity, her life as a monarch was not without serious challenges. One of the most startling facts about her reign is that she survived at least eight assassination attempts.

The first attempt on her life happened in 1840, just four months after she married Prince Albert. At that time, Victoria was also four months pregnant with their first child. An 18-year-old man named Edward Oxford tried to shoot her while she was riding in a carriage. Fortunately, he missed, and Victoria was unharmed. Oxford was captured and spent 24 years in prison before being sent to Australia.

But this was not the only time Victoria faced danger. Over the years, other people tried to harm her, with attempts being made during different periods of her life, especially in the 1840s. The last known attempt occurred in 1882, over 40 years after the first one. During this incident, a group of students from Eton College saw the gunman and quickly sprang into action, using their umbrellas to stop him before he could do any harm.

Despite these frightening experiences, Queen Victoria remained strong and continued to fulfill her duties as queen, earning the respect and admiration of her people.

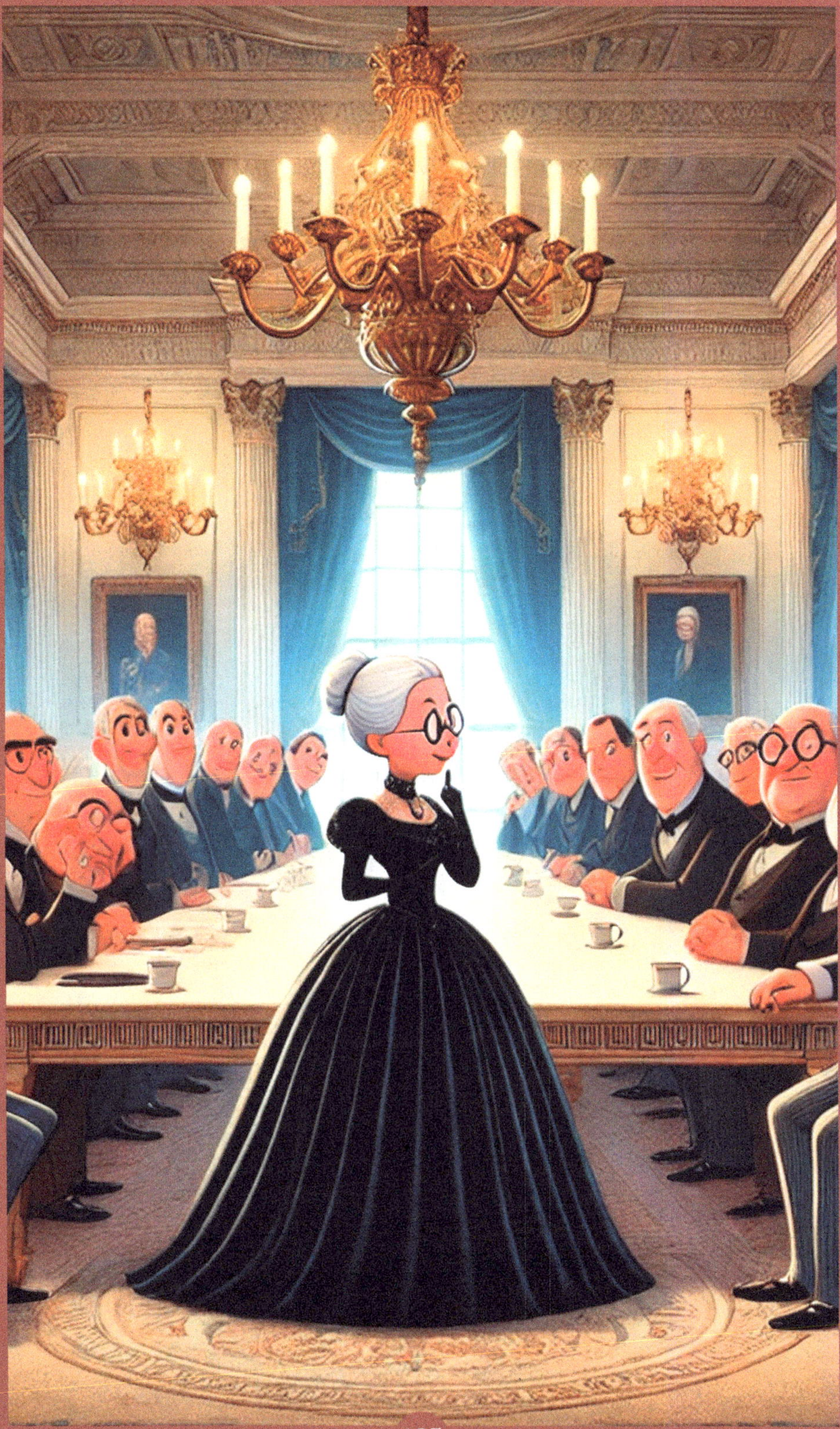

Queen Victoria's Resistance to Feminism - Even though Queen Victoria was one of the most powerful women in history, she didn't support the feminist movements that were growing during her time. These movements, led by women known as suffragettes, fought for women's rights, including the right to vote. Victoria had strong opinions against these ideas. She called the suffragettes' efforts "mad, wicked folly" and believed that a woman's main role was in the home, caring for her family. Despite being a female ruler, she thought that women should focus on being good wives and mothers rather than seeking equality in politics or other areas outside the home. This view was quite different from what many feminists were fighting for at the time.

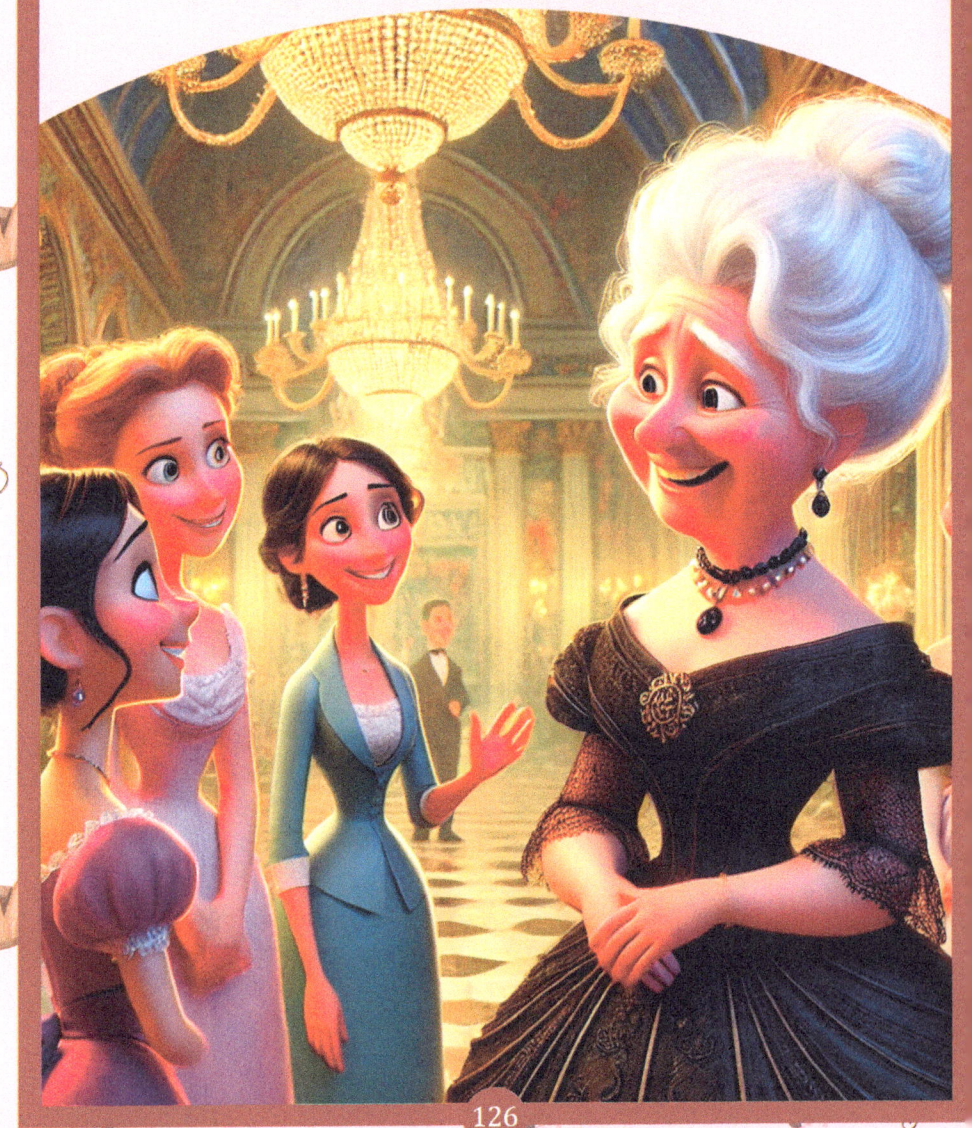

Queen Victoria's Global Legacy - Queen Victoria was so influential that many places around the world were named after her. This shows how much people admired her and how far the British Empire reached during her reign.

One of the most famous places is the state of Queensland in Australia, named in her honor. Victoria Falls, one of the largest and most spectacular waterfalls in the world, is located on the border between Zambia and Zimbabwe in Africa and also carries her name. In Canada, the capital city of British Columbia is called Victoria. Even in Greece, there is a place called Victoria Square in Athens, named after this famous British queen.

These names are a reminder of Queen Victoria's lasting impact and how she is remembered in many different countries around the world.

Queen Victoria's Obsession with Mourning -Queen Victoria's grief after the death of her beloved husband, Prince Albert, was so deep that it became a central part of her life. Her mourning went far beyond just wearing black clothing, which she did for the rest of her life.

Victoria was so heartbroken that she insisted on keeping Albert's memory alive in very personal and specific ways. She had his rooms maintained exactly as they were when he was alive, as if he might return at any moment. Every day, his clothes were laid out, and a hot water bath was prepared for him, just as it had been when he was alive. These daily rituals were a way for Victoria to feel close to Albert, even though he was gone. Her intense and lifelong mourning showed just how much she loved him and how deeply his loss affected her.

The Final Years and Legacy

"Kindness in words creates confidence."
Queen Victoria

As the years went by, Queen Victoria grew older, and her once-boundless energy began to wane. She had ruled for a very long time, and though her body was growing weaker, her spirit remained as strong as ever. Even in her final years, Victoria was deeply committed to her role as Queen. She knew that her people still looked to her for guidance and strength, and she was determined to continue serving them for as long as she could. Victoria's health began to decline, and she often felt tired and frail. But despite this, she never stopped working. She still met with her advisors, read important documents, and made decisions for her country. Her love for her people and her sense of duty kept her going, even when she was not feeling well.

In 1897, something remarkable happened—Victoria celebrated her Diamond Jubilee, marking 60 years on the throne. This was an extraordinary milestone, and once again, the entire country came together to celebrate their beloved queen. People from all corners of the British Empire came to London to join in the festivities. The streets were filled with joy, as crowds gathered to honor the woman who had led them for so long.

Victoria was deeply moved by the celebrations. Although she was now in her late seventies, the love and admiration of her people brought a warm smile to her face. The Diamond Jubilee was a grand occasion, with parades, parties, and fireworks lighting up the sky. Victoria rode through the streets in a carriage, just as she had during her Golden Jubilee ten years earlier. The people cheered and waved, their voices filled with love and gratitude for their queen. As she looked out at the cheering crowds, Victoria felt an overwhelming sense of pride. She thought about all the years that had passed, the challenges she had faced, and the progress her country had made. She knew that she had done her best to be a good queen, and she was grateful for the unwavering support of her people. After the Diamond Jubilee, Victoria's health continued to decline, and she grew weaker with each passing day. But even as her body grew frail, her mind remained sharp, and she continued to fulfill her duties as queen for as long as she could. She spent her final years surrounded by her family, who loved her dearly and cared for her with great tenderness.

On January 22, 1901, Queen Victoria passed away at the age of 81. The news of her death spread quickly, and there was a great outpouring of grief across Britain and the world. People mourned the loss of their queen, who had been a constant presence in their lives for so many years. But along with the sadness, there was also a deep sense of respect and admiration for all that Victoria had achieved during her reign. Victoria had been queen for 63 years, the longest reign of any British monarch at that time. Her reign had seen incredible changes, from the growth of the British Empire to advances in industry, technology, and culture. She had led her country with grace, strength, and unwavering dedication, and her impact was felt far beyond the borders of Britain. Even after her passing, Queen Victoria's legacy lived on. She was remembered not just as a queen, but as a symbol of an era—the Victorian Era—that was marked by progress, innovation, and a deep sense of duty. Her name became synonymous with the values she held dear: hard work, responsibility, and a love for her people.

Queen Victoria's legacy also lived on through her many descendants, who went on to play important roles in the royal families of Europe. She became known as the "Grandmother of Europe" because so many of her children and grandchildren married into other royal families.

But more than anything, Victoria was remembered as a queen who truly cared for her people. She had faced many challenges in her life, from the loss of her beloved Albert to the responsibilities of leading a vast empire. Yet through it all, she had remained strong, dedicated, and compassionate. Queen Victoria's reign was a shining example of what it means to be a leader. She showed the world that true strength comes not just from power, but from love, kindness, and a deep commitment to those you serve. And so, even though she was no longer with them, the people of Britain and the world continued to hold her memory close to their hearts, remembering her as one of the greatest monarchs in history. Victoria's legacy would live on forever, in the hearts of her people, in the history books, and in the very fabric of the nation she had loved and served so well.

Fascinating Facts about Queen Victoria:

Queen Victoria's Hidden Talents - Queen Victoria had some surprising talents that not everyone knows about. She was a skilled artist who loved to draw and paint. Over her lifetime, she created hundreds of sketches and watercolors, often capturing scenes of her family and the beautiful surroundings at her Scottish home, Balmoral Castle. Her artwork shows that she had a great eye for detail and a deep love for her family and nature. In addition to her artistic abilities, Queen Victoria was a dedicated diarist. She kept detailed journals throughout her life, starting when she was just a young girl. These journals are filled with her thoughts, feelings, and observations about the events happening around her. They give us a personal look into what it was like to be a queen during a time of great change and how Victoria felt about the many important events in her life. Her diaries are still read today by historians who want to understand more about this famous queen.

Queen Victoria and Hemophilia - Queen Victoria carried a rare genetic condition called hemophilia B, which affects the blood's ability to clot. Although Victoria herself did not suffer from this disorder, she passed the gene to her descendants. Hemophilia B is known for causing excessive bleeding, even from minor injuries, because the blood doesn't clot properly.

Because Queen Victoria had many children and grandchildren, the gene spread through many royal families across Europe. This meant that several members of royal and noble families were affected by this condition. A 2009 study published in Science Magazine found that the hemophilia mutation was also present in the Russian royal family, the Romanovs.

The impact of this condition on Victoria's family was significant. Her son, Leopold, the Duke of Albany, died at the young age of 30 after a fall, which led to severe bleeding. Two of her grandsons, Friedrich and Leopold, also tragically died because of the disorder.

The last known royal carrier of hemophilia B was Prince Waldemar of Prussia, who passed away in 1945. Queen Victoria's genetic legacy had a lasting effect on many royal families, highlighting how one person's genetic trait can influence history across generations.

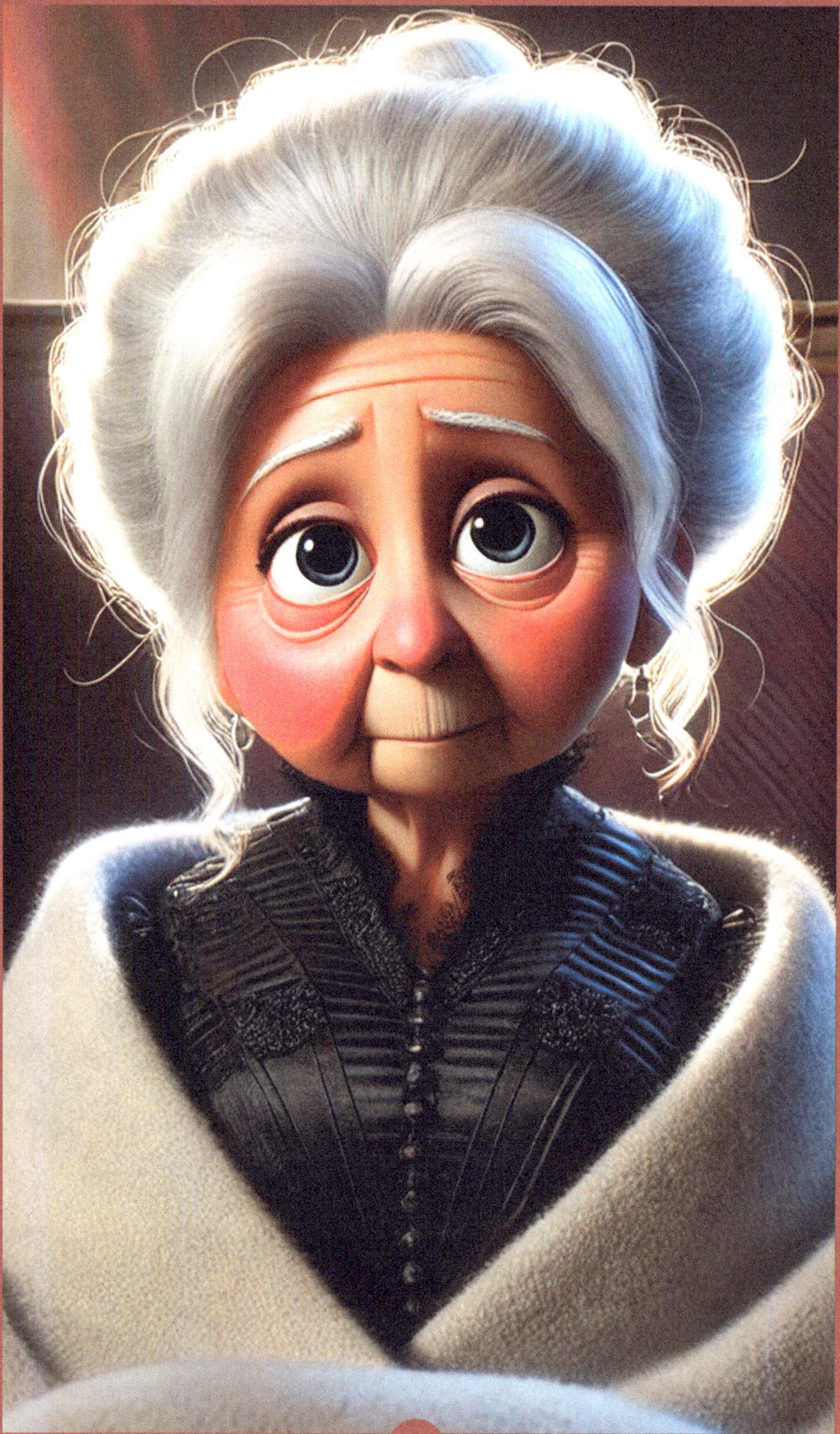

Queen Victoria's Train Ride - During the Victorian era, when new technologies were changing the world, Queen Victoria experienced one of the latest innovations: the train. In 1842, Victoria became the very first British monarch to ride a train.

At 23 years old, she took a journey from Slough, near Windsor Castle, to Paddington in West London. The trip was quite short, taking about 30 minutes.

Victoria was very pleased with the ride. She found it much more comfortable than traveling by carriage. She remarked that the train's movement was smooth, and there was no dust or heat, which made the journey pleasant. This ride was not just a personal experience for Victoria but also a sign of how the new railways were becoming an important part of life in Britain.

Queen Victoria's Impact on Medicine - Queen Victoria played an important role in changing the way medicine was practiced, especially during childbirth. When she gave birth to her eighth child, she became one of the first women in Britain to use chloroform as a pain relief method. At the time, using anesthesia during childbirth was controversial, with many people believing it was unnatural or even dangerous.

However, Queen Victoria's positive experience with chloroform helped to change people's minds. Her use of the anesthetic made it more acceptable for other women to use during childbirth. As a result, chloroform and other forms of pain relief became more widely used, making childbirth a bit easier and less painful for many women. Queen Victoria's decision had a lasting impact on medicine and helped pave the way for modern childbirth practices.

Queen Victoria's Final Rest - After a long and eventful life, Queen Victoria passed away in January 1901 at the age of 81. Her death marked the end of an era known as the Victorian Era, a time of great change and influence in Britain and beyond.

Victoria was laid to rest beside her beloved husband, Prince Albert, in a special place called Frogmore Mausoleum. This mausoleum is located near Windsor, where it's peaceful and surrounded by beautiful gardens. Being buried alongside Albert, whom she loved deeply, was very important to Victoria.

Her final resting place at Frogmore Mausoleum is a place where people can remember and honor the legacy of Queen Victoria and her remarkable reign.

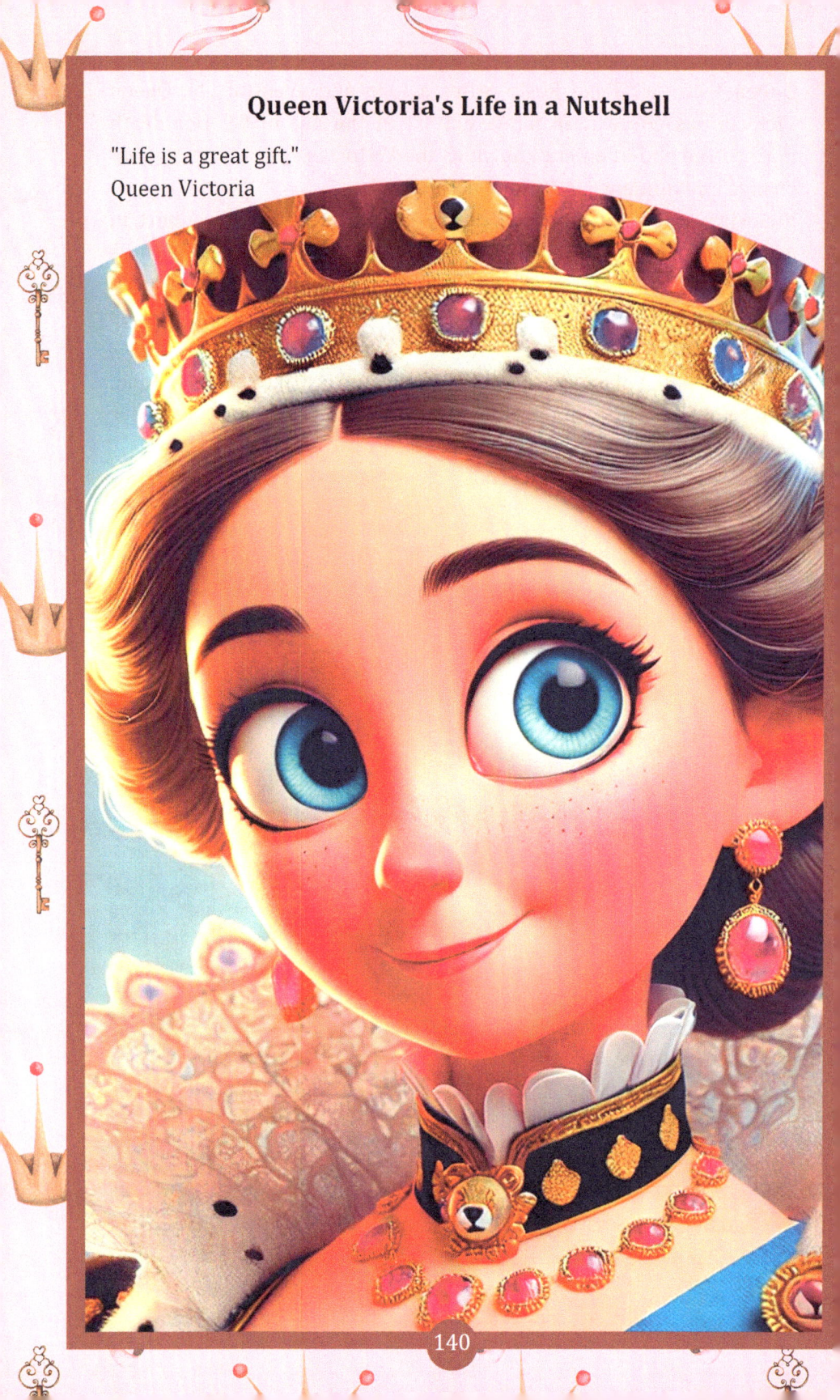

Queen Victoria's Life in a Nutshell

"Life is a great gift."
Queen Victoria

1819: Birth
• Victoria was born on May 24, 1819, in Kensington Palace, London, England. Her full name was Alexandrina Victoria, but she was called Victoria.

1837: Victoria Becomes Queen
• When Victoria was 18 years old, her uncle, King William IV, passed away. On June 20, 1837, Victoria became queen, starting her reign as the Queen of the United Kingdom.

1840: Marriage to Prince Albert
• On February 10, 1840, Queen Victoria married her cousin, Prince Albert of Saxe-Coburg and Gotha. They were very much in love and had nine children together.

1840-1861: Family Life
• Queen Victoria and Prince Albert had a happy family life. Their nine children married into royal families across Europe, which is why Victoria was often called the "Grandmother of Europe."

1861: Prince Albert Passes Away
• In 1861, Prince Albert passed away from typhoid fever. Victoria was heartbroken and wore black for the rest of her life to show that she was in mourning.

1877: Becoming Empress of India
• In 1877, Queen Victoria was given the title "Empress of India" as a way to strengthen ties between Britain and its colony, India. This showed how powerful the British Empire had become during her reign.

1887: Golden Jubilee

- In 1887, Victoria celebrated her Golden Jubilee, marking 50 years as queen. People all over the British Empire celebrated, and Victoria was honored with parades, banquets, and gifts.

1897: Diamond Jubilee

- Ten years later, in 1897, Victoria celebrated her Diamond Jubilee, marking 60 years on the throne. By this time, she was the longest-reigning monarch in British history.

1901: Queen Victoria Passes Away

- Queen Victoria passed away on January 22, 1901, at the age of 81. She had ruled for 63 years, which was longer than any British monarch before her.

Legacy

- Queen Victoria is remembered as one of Britain's greatest monarchs. Her reign, known as the Victorian Era, was a time of great progress in industry, science, and the arts. She helped shape modern Britain and left a lasting legacy through her many descendants and the expansion of the British Empire.

Queen Victoria
By: Reza Nazari

Copyright © 2024 Effortless Math Education, USA
All rights reserved.
No part of this publication may be reproduced, stored in a retrieval system, or transmitted in any form or by any means, electronic, mechanical, photocopying, recording, scanning, or otherwise, except as permitted under Section 107 or 108 of the 1976 United States Copyright Act, without permission of the author.
All inquiries should be addressed to:
www.Effortlessmath.com
info@Effortlessmath.com
Published by: Effortlessmath.com

Made in United States
Orlando, FL
25 March 2025